ALASKA WILDLIFE VIEWING GUIDE

MICHELLE SYDEMAN and ANNABEL LUND

FALCON™

Helena, Montana

CONTENTS

PROJECT SPONSORS

The ALASKA DEPARTMENT OF FISH AND GAME is charged with the maintenance, development, and enhancement of fish and wildlife resources in Alaska. It provides for the sustained optimum use of these resources, consistent with the social, cultural, aesthetic, environmental, and economic needs of the people. ADFG, 333 Raspberry Road, Anchorage, AK 99518. (907) 267-2351.

The U.S. DEPARTMENT OF DEFENSE is the steward of about 25 million acres of land in the United States; many areas possess irreplaceable natural and cultural resources. As our nation continues to grow and develop, these military lands become more important as last strongholds of dwindling wildlife resources. USAR, 600 Richardson Drive, No. 6500, Fort Richardson, AK 99505-6500. (907) 384-3046. Elemendorf AFB, 3 CES, USAF, 22040 Maple Street, Anchorage, AK 99503. (907) 522-2436.

The NATIONAL PARK SERVICE manages more than 54 million acres in Alaska—15 percent of Alaska's land. The mission of the agency is to conserve the scenery, natural and historic objects, and wildlife on park lands, providing for the enjoyment of present and future generations. NPS, 2525 Gambell St., Room 107, Anchorage, AK 99503. (907) 257-2475.

The mission of the U.S. FISH AND WILDLIFE SERVICE, which administers more than 77 million acres in Alaska, is to conserve, protect, and enhance fish and wildlife and their habitats. The agency also protects endangered and threatened species, conserves migratory birds, restores fisheries, enforces the law, and promotes education, recreation, and wildlife research. USFWS, 1011 E. Tudor Road, Anchorage, AK 99503. (907) 786-3542.

The FOREST SERVICE, U.S. Department of Agriculture, manages nearly 23 million acres of Alaska public land. The agency's mission is to protect, improve, and wisely use forest resources to meet the needs of current users and future generations. USFS, Naturewatch Program, P.O. Box 21628, Juneau, AK 99802-1628. (907) 586-8752.

The BUREAU OF LAND MANAGEMENT is responsible for 80 million acres of Alaska land. The BLM manages public land under principles of multiple use and sustained yield, balancing environmental protection, resource development, and recreation. BLM, 222 W. 7th Street, No. 13, Anchorage, AK 99513. (907) 271-5076.

The ALASKA DIVISION OF PARKS & OUTDOOR RECRE-ATION is charged with providing outdoor recreation opportunities, protecting and interpreting areas of natural and cultural significance, and supporting the state's tourism industry. ADP, 3601 C Street, Suite 1200, Anchorage, AK 99503-5921. (907) 269-8700.

The FEDERAL AID IN SPORT FISH AND WILDLIFE RESTORA-TION PROGRAM distributes funds to state fish and game agencies for restoration, conservation, and enhancement of sport fish and wildlife resources. These funds are collected from America's sportsmen and women, who pay a manufacturers' excise tax on angling, boating, and hunting gear. Federal Aid, 1011 E. Tudor Road, Anchorage, AK 99503. (907) 789-3435.

The ALASKA NATURAL HISTORY ASSOCIATION is an educational nonprofit organization that works with public land organizations to enhance the understanding and conservation of Alaska's natural, cultural, and historical resources. ANHA, 605 West 4th Street, Suite 85, Anchorage, AK 99501. (907) 274-8440.

DEFENDERS OF WILDLIFE is a national nonprofit organization of more than 100,000 members and supporters dedicated to preserving the natural abundance and diversity of wildlife and its habitat. A one-year membership is $20 and includes a subscription to *Defenders,* an award-winning conservation magazine. For further information, write or call Defenders of Wildlife, 1101 14th Street NW, Suite 1400, Washington DC 20005. (202) 682-9400.

The ALASKA VISITORS ASSOCIATION is a statewide, non-profit trade association promoting travel to and within the state of Alaska. AVA, 3201 "C" Street, Suite 403, Anchorage, AK 99503. (407) 561-5733.

The ALASKA WILDERNESS RECREATION AND TOURISM ASSOCIATION promotes the protection of Alaska's natural resources through ecologically responsible recreation and tourism. AWRTA, P.O. Box 1353, Valdez, AK. (907) 835-4300.

It is the mission of the ALASKA DIVISION OF TOURISM to create jobs and business opportunities for Alaskans; disperse the economic benefits of tourism throughout the state and the year; and assure an Alaska travel experience that is second to none. P.O. Box 110801, Juneau, AK 99811. (907) 465-2012.

ACKNOWLEDGMENTS

Funding for the research and development of this book was provided by the Alaska Department of Fish and Game and the U.S. Department of Defense. Without their commitment to conservation of wildlife and enhancement of wildlife viewing, this book would not exist.

Neither could this guide have been produced without the valuable assistance and insight of Liz Williams, John Schoen, Mark Schwan, Nancy Tankersley, Colleen Matt, John Wright, Ken Whitten, Mark Kirchoff, and Phil Koehl of the Alaska Department of Fish and Game. Thanks also to Cheryl Hull and Richard Carstensen.

We are indebted to the many site managers, biologists, and wildlife enthusiasts who gave of their time with patience and good humor to enhance the scope and accuracy of this project.

Numerous agencies and organizations helped in the research of this guide. In addition to the project sponsors, significant assistance was provided by the Alaska Department of Transportation and Public Facilities, Alaska Marine Highway System, the National Marine Fisheries Service, the Anchorage Division of Parks and Recreation, and the Sitka and Anchorage visitor and convention bureaus. Thanks also to the cities of Kotzebue and Barrow, and many of Alaska's Native regional and village corporations.

The guidance and expertise of the members of the Alaska Watchable Wildlife Steering Committee were valuable to the writers of this guide.

For each guide sold, one dollar will go to the Alaska Watchable Wildlife Conservation Trust managed by the Alaska Conservation Foundation for conservation, education, and wildlife viewing projects.

Authors
Michelle Sydeman and Annabel Lund
Alaska Department of Fish and Game

Project Manager
Michelle Sydeman

Illustrations
Paul Kratter

Front cover photo
Lon E. Lauber

Back cover photos
Brown bears: Tom Walker
Humpback whale: John Hyde

INTRODUCTION

After returning from his first visit to Alaska in 1899, geographer Henry Gannett cautioned, "If you are old, go by all means, but if you are young, stay away. . . . The scenery of Alaska is so much grander than anything else of the kind in the world . . . It is not well to dull one's capacity for such enjoyment by seeing the finest first."

We hope you disregard his warning. Alaska awaits you.

It is hard to describe the 49th state because, for most of us, there is nothing in our experience with which to compare it. Superimposed on a map of the "Lower 48," Alaska stretches from San Diego to Savannah. It has three times the coastline of the rest of the United States put together and is home to many of the tallest mountains, longest rivers, and largest lakes in the world. It has glaciers, forests, and parklands bigger than entire states.

In these magnificent settings, Alaska offers superb wildlife viewing opportunities. Bald eagles, caribou, and grizzly bears, driven away from other lands by the crush of modern development, roam wild and free. Walrus, muskoxen, and polar bears, which simply do not exist elsewhere in the nation, flourish. Species thrive undisturbed in their rich, natural habitats.

This spectacular and untamed country will be enjoyed most by those who recognize that new experiences are essential for a well-lived life. In Alaska, you may discover new truths about yourself and find nourishment in the marvels you encounter. You may not be the same person you were before climbing these mountains, hiking this tundra, paddling these rivers, and embracing these new horizons.

Although many of these sites are remarkably accessible, some demand a significant investment on the part of the traveler. We hope this guide will illustrate that the rewards of those efforts are great. And even if your only means of travel to Alaska are this book and a comfortable armchair, we hope this guide will provide landscapes for your dreams.

VIEWING HINTS

Choose your season. Many species of wildlife appear only during certain seasons at any given site. They may hibernate in the winter, migrate during the spring, or use special nesting areas during the summer. Check site write-ups and call site managers for detailed information before you go.

Dawn and dusk are the best times to view most wildlife. Areas that are barren of wildlife at midday may have been teeming with various kinds of animals during the early morning. Those who arrive early and stay late see more wildlife.

Learn the feeding habits of your quarry. Many shorebirds, marine birds, and waterfowl follow the tides in their daily feeding cycle. Other wildlife, including bears, spend large amounts of time during the summer near salmon streams and berry patches. Knowing the feeding habits of animals will help you to find them.

Use binoculars or a spotting scope. These tools will open a new world of wildlife viewing. For instance, with a 20-power spotting scope mounted on a tripod, it is possible to watch the activity of a mountain goat standing 1.5 miles away.

Move slowly and quietly. The best thing you can do to improve your chances of seeing wildlife is to slow down and stop periodically. Animals often disappear as you arrive but may return shortly if you are quiet enough. Use your ears to locate birds. Use your peripheral vision to spot movements in trees, thick brush, and water.

Fade into the woodwork. Wear natural colors and unscented lotions. Hide behind vegetation or boulders. Relax your muscles and avoid staring; animals can easily detect tension and may interpret a direct stare as a threat.

Look for animal sign. Tracks in the mud or snow, unusual scents, vegetation that has been recently browsed, and scat are all clues that wildlife has been in the area. Look for these clues as a way to find animals or appreciate them when they're out of sight.

Use field guides. Many good field guides are available to help identify mammals, birds, fish, and other fauna and flora. Knowing what you're looking at greatly enhances your viewing pleasure. Check "Suggested Reading and Reference Books" on page 94 for a list of guides.

Ask an expert. Some viewing areas have on-site staff. Don't be afraid to ask for advice. It can often make the difference between a disappointing visit and one you will remember forever.

Be patient. Allow yourself enough time in the field. Even in Alaska, where wildlife is abundant, it can take years, if not a lifetime, to see all the species listed in this guide.

VIEWING ETHICS

Give wildlife plenty of space. Binoculars and spotting scopes allow you to view wildlife without getting too close. Approach wildlife slowly, quietly, and indirectly. Always give animals an avenue for retreat.

Try to view animals without changing their behavior. Avoid using calls or devices that attract wildlife. Resist the temptation to throw rocks to see a flock fly. Remember—harassing wildlife is illegal.

Be respectful of nesting and denning areas, rookeries, and calving grounds. Well-meaning but intrusive visitors may cause parents to flee, leaving young vulnerable to the elements or predators. Stay on designated trails whenever possible.

Leave "orphaned" or sick animals alone. Young animals that appear alone usually have parents waiting nearby.

Restrain pets or leave them at home. They may startle, chase, or even kill wildlife.

Let animals eat their natural foods. Sharing your sandwich may get animals hooked on handouts; it may even harm their digestive systems. These animals may eventually lose their fear of cars, campers, or even poachers.

Learn to recognize signs of alarm. These are sometimes subtle. Leave if an animal shows them.

THE NATIONAL WATCHABLE WILDLIFE PROGRAM

The National Watchable Wildlife Program was established in 1990 by a consortium of federal land management agencies and national conservation groups, as well as the International Association of Fish and Wildlife Agencies.

Wildlife plays a crucial role in Alaska's economic, environmental, and spiritual well-being. Alaskans have always been aware of the importance of conservation. Wildlife is the warp and habitat the woof of the tapestry of the Alaska wilderness; we know that if threads are pulled out, the whole fabric may unravel. The Watchable Wildlife Program will help heighten public awareness and understanding of wildlife and their habitat and thus preserve and enhance Alaska's rich and unique biological heritage.

HOW TO USE THIS GUIDE

This guide is divided into five regions. The map that introduces each section lists and locates wildlife viewing sites within that region. Every site description contains the following elements.

The site number corresponds with the number on the map at the start of each region. The **description** section gives the lay of the land; it offers an overview of the habitats found at each site, and names specific species to look for. A **viewing information** section follows, and may include descriptions of the reliability of viewing, the best viewing seasons for selected species, local weather and road conditions, and the facilities available at the site. Specific viewing locales within site boundaries are offered when possible. IMPORTANT NOTES CONCERNING SITE RESTRICTIONS, SAFETY, AND VIEWING CONDITIONS ARE NOTED IN CAPITAL LETTERS.

Written **directions** are supplied for each viewing site; in some cases this section simply lists means of access to the site. The name of the **closest town** appears beneath the directions. Visitors should supplement the directions in this guide with an up-to-date state map, road atlas, county road map, or, in some cases, a topographic map.

Contact supplies the name of at least one agency responsible for managing the site and a telephone number for further information. **Recreation icons** appear at the bottom of each site account and offer an idea of the services available. This list should not be relied on exclusively; check with the site.

Alaska is a unique and challenging state. Viewers should plan their outings carefully in order to ensure a fulfilling and safe adventure.

Agency Abbreviations

ADF&G	Alaska Department of Fish and Game
ASP	Alaska State Parks
ADOTPF	Alaska Department of Transportation and Public Facilities
BLM	Bureau of Land Management
MOA	Municipality of Anchorage
NMFS	National Marine Fisheries Service
NPS	National Park Service
PVT	Private ownership, including Native corporations
USFS	U.S. Forest Service
USFWS	U.S. Fish and Wildlife Service

ALASKA
WILDLIFE VIEWING AREAS

Alaska's wildlife viewing sites have been organized into five viewing regions shown on this map. Within each region, sites are numbered consecutively in a general pattern. Each viewing region begins with a detailed map showing major roads and cities and the location of each wildlife viewing site.

FACILITIES & RECREATION

P Parking	**♿** Restrooms	**$** Entry Fee	**🥾** Hiking
X-Skiing	**🚲** Bicycling	Boat Ramp	Small Boats
Large Boats	**⛺** Camping	**🏕** Picnic	**🛏** Lodging
Restaurant	**♿** Barrier-free	Horse Trails	Historical or Cultural Significance
Public Use Cabin	**✈** Airport		

HIGHWAY SIGNS

As you travel in Alaska and other states, look for these signs on highways and other roads. They identify the route to follow to reach wildlife viewing sites.

WILDLIFE VIEWING AREA

BERING SEA

FAR NORTH

67
65
Kotzeb
Kotzeb

68
Nome

59
Bethel

60

57

SOUTHWEST ALASKA

58

ALASKA MARINE HIGHWAY SYS

16

PACIFIC OCEAN

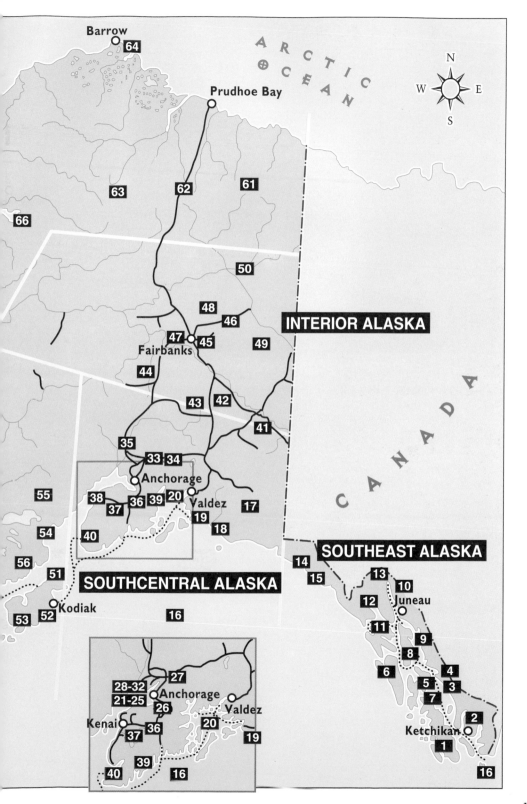

Barrow
64

ARCTIC OCEAN

Prudhoe Bay

N
W E
S

63   62   61

66

50

48
46   INTERIOR ALASKA
47 45
Fairbanks   49

44

43   42

41

CANADA

35

33 34
Anchorage
38   20
37 36 39 Valdez   17
19
40   18   SOUTHEAST ALASKA

55   14

54   15
56   13 10
51   12 Juneau
Kodiak   SOUTHCENTRAL ALASKA   11
53 52   16   9
8
6   4
5   3
27   7
28-32
21-25 Anchorage   2
26   Valdez
Kenai   20   Ketchikan
37 36   19   1
39
40   16   16

11

ALASKA'S 10 MOST WANTED

Wildlife watching is one of the main reasons people visit Alaska. And while hundreds of species can be seen and enjoyed, there are a few that are on the top of just about everyone's want-to-see list. Here you'll find the 10 species that almost everyone would like to see, plus information about habitat and behavior, viewing tips, and where and when you're most likely to find them.

JOHN HYDE

Bald Eagle (*Haliaeetus leucocephalus*)

Habitat: Throughout Alaska, except the Far North; especially plentiful along the coast in Southeast and Southcentral Alaska.

Viewing tips: Eagles congregate around waterfront food sources, particularly in places where fish are spawning or schooling, and are most active in the early morning. Hot spots include the Chilkat River Valley (late October to December); the Stikine River Flats (spring); and Admiralty Island and Prince William Sound (summer).

Fantastic facts: Bald eagles weigh up to 15 pounds and have 7-foot wing spans. About 30,000 bald eagles—the largest population in the U.S.—make Alaska their home. Eagles mate for life and may return to the same nest year after year. The eyesight of these birds is so good that they can spot a single fish from a mile away.

Brown (*Ursus arctos*) and Black Bear (*Ursus americanus*)

Habitat: Black bears are found in forests; inland brown bears (commonly known as grizzlies) generally in open, treeless areas; coastal brown bears in forested and mountainous areas.

Viewing tips: Bears are most commonly seen during evening hours, feeding on vegetation in late spring and fishing for salmon in summer and early fall. Look for them on beaches, in alpine tundra, and in lush subalpine meadows.

Fantastic facts: Black bears—despite their name—can range in color from light cinnamon to blue-gray; brown bears range from blond to black. Adult black bears range in weight from 200 to 500 pounds; brown bears may grow as large as 1,500 pounds. A brown bear is distinguished from a black bear by a characteristic hump over its shoulders; long, straight front claws; and a sometimes concave face.

ALISSA CRANDALL

LON E. LAUBER

Caribou *(Rangifer tarandus)*

Habitat: Arctic tundra and alpine tundra near or above the timberline; taiga forests in winter.

Viewing tips: Wildlife viewers can easily find small numbers of caribou to watch; viewing large numbers generally requires the use of aircraft, since Alaska's largest herds inhabit remote, roadless areas of the state. Hot spots are the northern section of the Dalton Highway, Denali National Park, the Denali Highway, the Richardson Highway between Sourdough and Paxson Lake (August, September, October, and April); the Glenn Highway near Eureka (winter); the Alaska Highway between Tok and the Canadian border (November to March); and the Kenai River Flats (mid-April to mid-October).

Fantastic facts: Alaska is home to nearly a million caribou in 32 herds. Caribou travel greater distances each year than any other land mammal—up to 3,000 miles. Their large, concave hooves spread wide to support them in snow and soft tundra and function as paddles when they swim. Newborn calves can walk within an hour of birth and can outrun a person within several days. When startled, caribou hop on their hind feet, emitting a scent to alert other caribou that danger may be imminent.

TOM WALKER

Dall Sheep *(Ovis dalli)*

Habitat: Open, alpine ridges; meadows; steep slopes with rugged cliffs.

Viewing tips: The best time to observe sheep is during May and June, when they descend to the snow-free slopes of lower elevations. Observe which way sheep are traveling and let them graze toward you. Hot spots include Denali National Park; Cooper Landing on the Kenai Peninsula; Atigun Pass on the Dalton Highway; and Windy Corner on the Seward Highway.

Fantastic facts: Male Dall sheep have massive curling horns, the rings of which can be counted to determine age. Ewes and rams live in separate bands and seldom associate, except during the mating season. Rams clash horns to establish dominance. The sound of the impact can often be heard a mile away. To protect themselves, the male sheep have skulls an inch thick over their brains.

Humpback Whale (*Megaptera novaeangliae*)

Habitat: Nearshore waters along the southern coast of Alaska.

Viewing tips: Look for the clouds of vapor humpbacks force from their blowholes as they surface and exhale, and listen for the explosive whooshing sound. When humpbacks dive, they often lift their flukes (tails) out of the water. In Alaska, the largest concentrations of humpbacks are in Southeast, in Prince William Sound, near Kodiak and Barren Islands, between Semidi and Shumagin Islands, in the eastern Aleutians, and in the southern Bering Sea.

Fantastic facts: These massive sea mammals have the capacity to stay submerged for up to 30 minutes. Females average 35 tons; males 25; newborns 2. Most Alaska humpbacks spend the winter near Hawaii, where they bear young. Humpbacks often feed cooperatively, herding their prey, exhaling columns of bubbles to concentrate it, and lunging to the surface with their mouths wide open. Ventral grooves allow the whale's throat to expand and take in a large volume of water, which the whale then forces out across baleen plates that retain food. More than 23,000 whales were taken in the North Pacific before whaling was banned in 1966. Scientists estimate that between 1,000 and 1,200 humpbacks are alive today.

Moose (*Alces alces*)

Habitat: Spruce forests; freshwater marshes; willow thickets; Interior river valleys.

Viewing tips: Look for browsing areas in the early morning and at twilight, especially along highways where roads are close to rivers and ponds. Moose are commonly seen in the Mat-Su Valley, on the Kenai Peninsula, and in the Anchorage Bowl.

Fantastic facts: Weighing up to 1,600 pounds, moose are the largest deer in the world. They can run at speeds up to 35 mph and can swim at 6 mph for up to two hours. During the breeding season (or "rut"), males joust with one another by bringing their massive antlers together and pushing. Cows with calves can be fiercely protective; don't come between them. Moose are prized by hunters for their delicious meat; Alaskans harvest 6,000 to 8,000 annually.

MICHAEL DeYOUNG

Muskox (*Ovibos moschatus*)

Habitat: Arctic tundra; grassy river valleys, lakeshores, and meadows in summer; windswept hilltops and slopes where vegetation is exposed in winter.

Viewing tips: Wild herds can be seen on Nelson and Nunivak Islands, on the Seward Peninsula, on the coastal plain of the Arctic National Wildlife Refuge, and occasionally along the Dalton Highway north of Atigun Pass.

Fantastic facts: Muskoxen gather in small herds; when threatened, they form a fortresslike circle around their young. These shaggy creatures have changed little since the Ice Age. Adults weigh 600 to 900 pounds. When in rut, males battle for mates, charging each other at top speed from 50 yards; their violent collisions can be heard a mile away. Roughly 2,500 muskoxen range free in Alaska. Inupiaq-speaking Eskimos call the muskox "omingmak," which means "bearded one."

Puffin: Horned (*Fratercula corniculata*) and Tufted (*Fratercula cirrhata*)

Habitat: Coastal islands and headlands during breeding season; marine waters in winter.

Viewing tips: The best viewing is in summer. Look on steep, grassy slopes and cliffs near the top of established seabird colonies. Hot spots include the Pribilof Islands, Glacier Bay, the Kenai Fjords, St. Lawrence Island, Gull Island in Kachemak Bay, St. Lazaria Island, the Barren Islands, and Walrus Islands in Bristol Bay.

Fantastic facts: Dubbed "sea parrots" by early sailors, these enchanting birds have large colorful beaks and comical looks. They swim underwater using their wings to propel them and their webbed feet to steer. Tufted puffins nest in burrows 3 to 4 feet underground, which they dig with their sharp claws. Horned puffins nest in crevices on cliffs or rocky slopes. Historically, Alaska Natives used puffins for food and clothing. Though puffins are abundant in Alaska, their numbers have declined in the Lower 48 due to pollution and fishery conflicts.

K. R. WHITTEN

TOM WALKER

Sea Otter (*Enhydra lutris*)

Habitat: Shallow coastal waters from Southeast Alaska to the Aleutian Islands.

Viewing tips: Look in protected bays and inlets, especially near kelp beds. Mothers often anchor their young in kelp while foraging. Check rocks in the tidal zone during low tide for hauled-out otters. Hot spots include Prince William Sound, the outside coast of Southeast Alaska, Kachemak Bay, Kodiak Island, and the Kenai Fjords.

Fantastic facts: Sea otters eat as much as 25 percent of their body weight daily. They collect clams, crabs, and mussels, pile them on their chests and crack them open using small rocks. When not busy feeding, mothers rest their pups on their bellies while they float on their backs. Often called "old men of the sea," otters played a critical role in the Russian settlement and, ultimately, sale of Alaska. Demand for their luxurious fur nearly led to their extinction. Today, Alaska is home to more than 100,000 of them, roughly 90 percent of the world's sea otter population.

JOHN HYDE

Wolf (*Canis lupus*)

Habitat: A wide variety of habitats from the temperate rainforest of Southeast Alaska to arctic tundra.

Viewing tips: Look in large, open river beds and tundra areas. Search for tracks in soft soil and snow. From mid-May through August, most wolves center their activities around den and rendezvous sites. They are usually active during the early morning and evening. Listen for wolf howls, especially during the breeding season in February and March. Hot spots include the northern mountains and foothills of the Brooks Range, the Alaska Range (including Denali National Park), and the Chugach, Wrangell, and Talkeetna Mountains.

Fantastic facts: Wolves may eat 20 pounds of meat at a time, then go for a week without food. They are able to travel great distances, occasionally covering more than 40 miles during a day-long hunting expedition. Historically, wolves inhabited nearly the entire land mass of North America and Eurasia, a larger area than any other mammal except the Pleistocene lion. They are thought to mate for life. An estimated 8,700 wolves live in Alaska.

REGION ONE:
SOUTHEAST ALASKA

Alaska Marine Highway System
Primary Roads
Secondary Roads

14 Yakutat 15

13 HAINES

12

Gustavus 11 Hoonah

1. Prince of Wales Island
2. Misty Fjords National Monument
3. Stikine River Flats
4. LeConte Bay
5. Blind Slough Complex
6. Sitka: Starrigavan, Beaver Lake,
   Whale Park
7. Anan Creek
8. Pack Creek: Stan Price State Wildlife
   Sanctuary
9. Tracy Arm
10. Mendenhall Wetlands State Game
    Refuge
11. Icy Strait
12. Glacier Bay National Park and
    Preserve
13. Alaska Chilkat Bald Eagle Preserve
14. Summit Lake/Tawah Creek
15. Situk River: Nine Mile Bridge
16. Alaska Marine Highway

The lives of those in Southeast Alaska, which encompasses the largest temperate old-growth rainforest in North America, are inextricably linked with the sea. Offshore, pristine waters are rich with marine life, providing economic, cultural, and emotional sustenance to those who inhabit the snug towns and villages of the Inside Passage. Bear and deer live in the heart of ancient forests of towering spruce and hemlock; the woods' profound stillness punctuated by the clamor of hectic mountain streams, the haunting cry of bald eagles, and the captive thunder of calving glaciers. Mountain goats feed on the remote alpine tundra of the Southeast's steep and broken mountain ranges. Much of the ragged coastline is sheltered from the storm-tossed North Pacific; the crashing surf spends its violence against the seaward islands and is humbled into small waves that break gently on the pebbled and sandy beaches of the inside waters.

THE OLD-GROWTH RAINFOREST OF SOUTHEAST ALASKA

Ancient Sitka spruce and hemlock dominate the rainforest of Southeast Alaska, providing cover for abundant wildlife. Shown here from top to bottom, left to right: marbled murrelet, northern goshawk, Sitka black-tailed deer, brown bear, belted kingfisher, bald eagle, red-breasted merganser, arctic char, Dolly Varden, chum salmon, sockeye salmon, three-spined stickleback, and coho salmon.

1. PRINCE OF WALES ISLAND

Description: Prince of Wales is the third largest island in the U.S. Its northern end is honeycombed by karst—limestone terrane with caves, sinkholes, and disappearing streams. The island's forests support populations of Sitka black-tailed deer and black bear. Visitors may also catch a glimpse of the Alexander Archipelago wolf. One of the largest bald eagle populations in the world resides on Prince of Wales, and the island's caves are ideal habitat for bats. The island's fishing industries have established an international reputation; they have also built several viewing platforms and bridges from which visitors may observe spawning coho, chum, sockeye, and pink salmon. Mergansers, great blue herons, and belted kingfishers are often seen in the island's estuaries and freshwater habitats. The ocean's tide leaves its prints along a thousand miles of coastline. Saltwater habitats support generous populations of marbled murrelets, common murres, and pigeon guillemots. Orcas, humpback whales, Dall porpoises, sea and river otters, Steller sea lions, and harbor seals are at home in the sheltered coastal waters.

Viewing Information: An extensive system of logging roads was built to facilitate clearcutting of large portions of the commercially valuable forest. Only 30 miles of roadway are paved. Two karst caves, El Capitan and Cavern Lake, are open to visitors. The best bat viewing occurs near isolated ponds and riverbanks at dusk.

Directions: *The island can be reached by floatplane or ferry from Ketchikan.*

Contact: USFS (907) 826-3271; Thorne Bay (907) 828-3304

Size: More than 1.4 million acres

Closest Towns: Craig, Klawock, Hydaburg

Sitka black-tailed deer are native to the wet coastal rain forests of Southeast Alaska. Fawns weigh 6 to 8 pounds at birth and stand about 12 inches tall. They are born in the spring and keep their spotted coats through the summer.

TOM WALKER

21

2. MISTY FJORDS NATIONAL MONUMENT

Description: Craggy cliffs, snow-capped peaks, and old growth forests stand guard over a filigree of deep fjords; glacial forces were at work here. Western hemlock and Sitka spruce provide habitat for brown and black bears, Sitka black-tailed deer, and wolves. Mountain goats scramble across rocky promontories. Humpback whales and orcas, Steller sea lions, Dall porpoises, and harbor seals feed on the rich population of fish and other marine life. Bald eagles build their nests in huge cedar trees. Wilson's warblers, Pacific slope flycatchers, rufous hummingbirds, and Swainson's thrushes are all neotropical migrants to the area. Marbled murrelets live in the monument all year long, and the fjords provide important winter habitat for goldeneyes, buffleheads, and loons. As nonhuman as the landscape feels, it harbors traces of early human inhabitants: 10,000-year-old pictographs (images painted on rocks) and petroglyphs (images etched into rocks).

Viewing Information: Prepare for rain; the area gets an average of 150 inches annually. The driest months are April to August. Four open-style shelters are available on a first-come first-served basis, and 14 cabins on saltwater and freshwater lakes can be reserved for a small fee. The majority of the monument is a designated wilderness area. Conditions are rustic with only six miles of trails and very few developed sites.

Directions: The monument can be reached from the tiny town of Hyder (by small plane, ferry, or vehicle through Canada), from Ketchikan (by private vessel, charter boat, or floatplane), or from Prince Rupert (generally by private boat).

Contact: USFS (907) 225-2148   **Size:** 2.3 million acres

Closest Town: Ketchikan

Massive ice bodies, up to one mile thick, covered this area as recently as 10,000 years ago. As these glaciers receded, they scoured the mountain tops of vegetation and carved the deep fjords pictured here. JOHN HYDE

3. STIKINE RIVER FLATS

Description: The vast tidal flats of the Stikine River host one of the most magical gatherings of birds in Southeast Alaska. Millions of migratory birds stop here to rest and feed on their way north in the spring and south in the fall. Snow geese, Canada geese, trumpeter and tundra swans, mergansers, sandhill cranes, and countless numbers and varieties of shorebirds and ducks all touch down in this designated wilderness area. In the spring, a small, oily fish called eulachon (pronounced "hooligan" by locals) spawns in the sandy bottom of the Stikine River. The stranded eulachon provide a feast for bald eagles—as many as 1,500 perch in cottonwoods along the lower river or next to pools in the mudflats—as well as for harbor seals and Steller sea lions.

Viewing Information: The largest concentrations of shorebirds alight on the mudflats west and north of Mallard Slough from late April to mid-May. Snow geese are most abundant in mid-April, when watchers have counted as many as 15,000. The best time for "eulachon watching" is between late March and early May. Short-eared owls and northern harriers swoop low over the grassflats as they hunt rodents and birds. Goshawks, peregrine falcons, or merlins chase ducks and other birds. Scan willow thickets along the river for moose; check the river's muddy banks for wolf and bear tracks. Six public use cabins in the area may be reserved for a fee.

Directions: *Access to the Stikine Flats is limited to boats and floatplanes, which may be chartered in Wrangell and Petersburg. Travel depends on weather and tides.*

Contact: USFS (907) 874-2323; ADFG (907) 772-3801

Size: 23,000 acres

Closest Town: Wrangell

Migratory birds from as far away as South America rest and feed on these biologically rich tidal flats. The Stikine, which means "great river" in the local Tlingit language, runs 330 miles from British Columbia, Canada, to Southeast Alaska. JOHN HYDE

4. LECONTE BAY

Description: Granite cliffs rise from the silty waters of the bay and lead to the face of LeConte Glacier, the most southerly tidewater glacier on the Pacific coast. Local Tlingit Indians named the glacier "Hutli" after the mythical bird that creates thunder by flapping its wings. Huge bergs thunder down from the glacier to float silently in the still water. Hundreds of harbor seals bear pups on top of these frozen platforms. The pups are born in late May and June and stay with their mothers for about a month. During the pupping season, eagles circle overhead, eager to snatch any remains of the birthing process.

Viewing Information: Visitors entering LeConte Bay may see mountain goats on the hillsides, especially on Horn Cliffs. Black bears sometimes roam the beaches. July and August are the best times to view seals, after the sensitive pupping period. DO NOT APPROACH TOO CLOSE TO SEALS, ESPECIALLY WHEN YOUNG ARE PRESENT.

Directions: Tourboats leave from Petersburg and Wrangell.

Contact: USFS (907) 772-3871 or (907) 874-2323

Size: 7,040 acres

Closest Town: Petersburg

5. BLIND SLOUGH COMPLEX

Description: A visit to the Blind Slough complex is a ticket to a unique wilderness symphony: the beautiful and oddly musical calls of the trumpeter swans. The complex is a crucial stopover and wintering area for the stately birds. Hundreds of trumpeters pause to rest and feed on water plants on their journey south, and about 50 winter here before heading north again in the spring. The area is a good birding spot year-round

Viewing Information: Over 150 species of birds have been recorded in this area. Geese, mallards, hooded mergansers, and other waterfowl visit at the same time as the swans. Trumpeters can be seen from mid-October to April, with the best viewing opportunities in October and November. The Trumpeter Swan Observatory provides a covered viewing blind with interpretive signs. The ice-free Blind River Rapids are a critical feeding ground. Trumpeter swans are especially vulnerable to disturbance from late December to late February. Wildlife viewers are asked to use extreme caution. USE SPOTTING SCOPES AND BINOCULARS TO MAINTAIN A HEALTHY DISTANCE FROM THE FLOCKS, BE AS QUIET AS POSSIBLE, AND LEASH ALL PETS.

Directions: Travel from Petersburg on the Mitkof Highway. Blind River Rapids is at mile 14.2, the Trumpeter Swan Observatory is at mile 16.1, and the Crystal Lake Fish Hatchery is at mile 17.2.

Contact: USFS (907) 772-3871

Size: About 20 acres   **Closest Town:** Petersburg

6. SITKA: STARRIGAVAN, BEAVER LAKE, AND WHALE PARK

Description: The bird-viewing shelter at the Starrigavan Recreation Area allows visitors to see great blue herons, bald eagles, Steller's jays, and hundreds of songbirds, shorebirds, and seabirds. Commonly spotted birds include rufous hummingbirds, red-breasted sapsuckers, common mergansers, varied thrushes, and glaucous-winged gulls. A footbridge and viewing deck at Starrigavan Creek provide glimpses of spawning pink and coho salmon. Beaver Lake is one of the few places in Southeast Alaska from which to view arctic grayling. Whale Park, a brand new facility, has boardwalks and gazebos containing high-powered binoculars. These offer an unobstructed view of Eastern Channel and the mouth of Silver Bay, a winter feeding area for humpback whales and other marine mammals.

Viewing Information: Winter and spring are the best seasons to observe humpbacks from Whale Park. Spring, summer, and early fall are the best seasons for birding at Starrigavan. Accessible by wheelchair, the bird-viewing shelter is at the beginning of the Estuary Life Interpretive Trail. Salmon spawn in Starrigavan Creek from late August through September. Grayling spawn in Beaver Lake mid-May to early June. The best place to see them is the outlet stream to the left as the trail nears the lake. STAY ON THE TRAIL TO AVOID DISTURBING FISH OR DAMAGING THE STREAM BANK.

Directions: The Starrigavan bird-viewing shelter is 7.5 miles north of downtown Sitka on Halibut Point Road. To reach Beaver Lake, take Sawmill Creek Road south from Sitka, turn left onto the gravel Blue Lake Road across from the pulp mill, and drive to the Sawmill Creek Campground. Cross the foot bridge and follow signs to the trail. Whale Park is four miles east of town on Sawmill Creek Road.

Contact: USFS (907) 747-6671; Sitka Convention and Visitors Bureau (907) 747-5940

Size: Starrigavan: 150 acres; Beaver Lake and Sawmill Creek Campground: about 45 acres

Closest Town: Sitka

Great blue herons often nest in the upper reaches of tall trees. They are expert fishers, capturing their prey by remaining motionless or by slowly stalking and then striking rapidly with their bills.
JOHN HYDE

25

7. ANAN CREEK WILDLIFE VIEWING AREA

Description: Surrounded by the Tongass National Forest, Anan Creek is one of the best places in Alaska to see black bears. The creek supports one of the largest runs of pink salmon in Southeast, attracting a variety of wildlife, from black and brown bears to bald eagles and harbor seals. Not far from salt water, a cascading waterfall slows the migrating salmon, making them easy for bears to catch. A scenic trail begins at the mouth of Anan Bay, winds half a mile along the lagoon and creek, and ends at an observatory where visitors can watch bears feeding. A public cabin is available for overnight use; make reservations.

Viewing Information: Black bears are most commonly seen near the falls, where fish congregate. Be prepared to spend some time waiting. Bald eagles are plentiful on the creek during the salmon run; at low tide, look for them in the lagoon, where they feed on stranded fish and carcasses. The first bridge out from the trailhead is a good place to watch harbor seals herd schools of salmon against the rocks in pursuit of a meal. River otters, mink, and marten visit the creek, as well as gulls, ravens, crows, mergansers, belted kingfishers, dippers, and herons. The best time to visit is mid-July to mid-August. DRESS WARMLY, WEAR RUBBER BOOTS, AND LEAVE PETS AT HOME.

Directions: Anan is accessible only by boat or floatplane. Several charter companies offer trips from nearby communities, especially Wrangell and Ketchikan.

Contact: USFS (907) 874-2323

Size: 105 acres within the 17-million-acre Tongass National Forest

Closest Town: Wrangell

Black bears are the smallest of the North American bears. An average adult male weighs 250 to 300 pounds and measures about five feet from nose to tail. Black bears have been recorded in all states except Hawaii. ALISSA CRANDALL

8. PACK CREEK: STAN PRICE STATE WILDLIFE SANCTUARY

Description: Alaska Natives call Admiralty Island "Kootznoowoo"—the fortress of the bears. The sanctuary is named for Stan Price, "the bear man of Pack Creek," who lived for 40 years in harmony with the large brown bears he came to cherish. The huge bruins outnumber people on the island; the average density is one brown bear per square mile. Although bears are the main attraction, visitors also frequently see humpback whales, harbor seals, Sitka black-tailed deer, river otters, and dozens of species of birds, including great blue herons, ravens, marbled murrelets, belted kingfishers, Steller's jays, green-winged teal, and harlequin ducks. And, Admiralty Island boasts the world's highest concentration of nesting bald eagles.

Viewing Information: Access to Pack Creek is restricted; permits must be secured in advance. A one-mile trail through the woods leads to an observation tower on upper Pack Creek, a great photography site. Visitors must keep to this trail and a designated beach trail and sand spit. The bears are active in the summer and are most abundant in July and August when pink and chum salmon fill the creek. The best times to view them are morning and evening; the viewing area is open from 9 a.m. to 9 p.m. Camping is permitted only on nearby Windfall Island; campers must use a boat to reach the island. Rental canoes are available.

Directions: *Access is by floatplane or boat. Several commercial guide services are available in Juneau.*

Contact: ADF&G (907) 465-4327; USFS (907) 586-8751

Size: 60,800 acres

Closest Town: Juneau

During the peak of the season, visitors may see up to a dozen different brown bears from this observation tower. The bears, hungry after five to seven months hibernation, fish for chum and pink salmon.
JOHN HYDE/ADF&G

27

9. TRACY ARM

Description: When naturalist John Muir visited Tracy Arm in 1879, he lamented that "amid so crowded a display of novel beauty it was not easy to concentrate the attention long enough on any portion of it without giving more days and years than our lives can afford." Sheer rock plunges into narrow fjords studded with slabs of blue glacial ice. Tracy and Endicott Arms stretch from the glaciers to the open waters of Holkham Bay and Stephens Passage. Look for sign of wolves, minks, martens, and river otters along the timber fringe of Endicott Arm. In the heart of Endicott Arm and high against the vertical granite walls of Tracy Arm, mountain goats catch the eye with their fearless climbing escapades. Brown bears feed on salmon along creeks, black bears on mussels along the tidal zone. Bald eagles circle overhead. Hundreds of harbor seals doze atop drifting icebergs. Arctic terns, marbled murrelets, and pigeon guillemots thrive in this habitat.

Viewing Information: Access to the area is by floatplane or boat. Commercially guided tours are available. There are rudimentary hiking opportunities but no facilities. VISITORS SHOULD AVOID SCARING SEALS OFF THEIR ICY PERCHES, particularly during the spring pupping season. Young seals are born and first weaned atop the ice where they are protected from orcas, their natural predators.

Directions: *48 miles south of Juneau*

Contact: USFS (907) 586-8800

Size: 653,000 acres

Closest Town: Juneau

Harbor seals depend on remote, undisturbed reefs and icebergs to rest, give birth, or nurse their pups. They can dive to depths of more than 600 feet and remain submerged for as long as 20 minutes at a time.
JOHN HYDE

10. MENDENHALL WETLANDS STATE GAME REFUGE

Description: The refuge is a critical wetlands area preserved in the midst of an urban setting. Right in the state's capital, freshwater streams tumble down from the peaks to meet the saltwater wetlands that cradle north Gastineau Channel. The result is a rich and fertile environment that supports 140 species of birds, eight species of anadromous fish, and a dozen or so species of mammals, such as long-tailed voles and masked shrews. Mendenhall is one of the most popular wetlands areas in the nation on a per-capita basis; residents and visitors alike use the area for birding, hunting, hiking, cross-country skiing, fishing, horseback riding, boating, or simply stealing a moment of peace in the midst of a bustling community.

Viewing Information: People are drawn to the refuge primarily to view the thousands of birds frequenting the wetlands, feeding and resting on their migratory paths. Some, like bald eagles, great blue herons, and Canada geese, feed throughout the year along the shoreline. Peregrine falcons visit the area in the fall and winter. The largest number of birds can be seen during spring migration in April and May. In late July, southbound shorebirds stop here to feed on marine invertebrates. Waterfowl arrive in late August and September.

Directions: The refuge is in the center of Juneau. Two access points are off Egan Drive: a cul-de-sac parking area at mile 3 and a scenic view turnout at mile 6. Also enter the refuge just west of the airport at the end of Radcliffe Road, or at mile 8.5 on the North Douglas Highway.

Contact: ADF&G (907) 465-4359

Size: 3,800 acres

Closest Town: Juneau

Canada geese spend most of their time in flocks, except during nesting. Pairs mate for life. They produce five to six eggs per nest and raise their young as a family unit. Later families often combine to form "creches" guarded by several parents. JOHN HYDE/ ADF&G

11. ICY STRAIT

Description: Near the mouth of Glacier Bay, Icy Strait is a popular place to view humpback whales. More than forty patrol the strait each summer, feeding on herring and other schooling fish. Most spend the winter in tropical waters off Hawaii, then return to Alaska in late spring. Watch for them rising out of the water, exposing their white and black grooved undersides, and rolling backwards with a loud smack. Steller sea lions, bald eagles, orcas, Dall porpoises, marbled murrelets, and a host of other seabirds also feed in these fish-rich waters. Other humpback whale watching sites in Southeast include Chatham Strait, Frederick Sound, and Stephens Passage.

Viewing Information: Humpbacks are present in Southeast throughout the year, but the peak viewing period is from mid-June through August. Scan waters along shorelines for the vapor forced out of their blowholes as the whales exhale. Humpbacks make a variety of underwater sounds; listen with a hydrophone to add a new dimension to the viewing experience. Feeding humpbacks usually dive for 5 to 10 minutes, but they can remain underwater for up to 30 minutes. When a whale shows its flukes, it is usually going to make a long, deep dive. STAY 100 YARDS FROM WHALES TO AVOID DISTURBING THEM.

Directions: Visitors can kayak in the strait, sail, or take a charter boat from Gustavus, Hoonah, Elfin Cove, or Juneau. The state ferry passes through Icy Strait en route from Hoonah to Pelican. Several tour boats ply these waters as well.

Contact: NPS (907) 697-2230; NMFS (907) 586-7235

Size: 50 miles

Closest Towns: Gustavus, Hoonah, Elfin Cove

Humpback whales often feed cooperatively, forming a ring underwater and blowing bubbles as they spiral upwards. This net of bubbles concentrates prey, making it possible for these large-bodied creatures to scoop up great numbers of fish with a single lunge to the surface. JOHN HYDE

12. GLACIER BAY NATIONAL PARK AND PRESERVE

Description: Just 200 years ago, the shorelines of Glacier Bay were completely covered by ice. Today, the park contains twelve tidewater glaciers, countless fjords and inlets, and the towering, snow-capped mountains of the Fairweather Range. The landscape is still evolving from stark, glacier-scrubbed boulders to lush temperate rain forests. Nowhere is the story of plant succession more richly told. The bay is also home, in some cases seasonally, to many wildlife species, including humpback whales, orcas, black and brown bears, wolves, moose, mountain goats, harbor seals, and more than 200 species of birds.

Viewing Information: Humpback whales swim in the lower bay from June 1 to August 15. Look for spray from their blowholes and listen for the whooshing sound of their breathing. Harbor seals float on icebergs or swim quietly in the ice-cold water, especially in Johns Hopkins Inlet and along the north tip of North Marble Island. Tidal Inlet and Gloomy Knob are good places to look for mountain goats. Use binoculars to spot black bears along the beaches and brown bears in the open meadows in the upper bay. From May to late August, most ships visiting the bay pass by huge colonies of black-legged kittiwakes, tufted puffins, and pigeon guillemots nesting on cliff faces and rocky islands; look closely as the boat passes the Marble Islands and approaches Margerie Glacier. Ask a park naturalist for help identifying some of the area's most interesting birds, including black oystercatchers, harlequin ducks, Kittlitz' murrelets, and surf scoters.

Directions: Glacier Bay is accessible by commercial cruise ship, tour boat, charter boat or aircraft, and by scheduled air and boat service from Juneau and other Southeast Alaska communities. Arrange flightseeing and boat trips into the bay at park headquarters. Kayaks can be rented in Bartlett Cove.

Contact: NPS (907) 697-2230

Size: 3.3 million acres   **Closest Town**: Gustavus

Muir Glacier has receded nearly 25 miles since John Muir studied it in 1890. Glaciers form when snowfall exceeds snowmelt and single flakes are pressed into solid ice by the weight of the accumulating snow. Four percent of Alaska is covered by ice.

GLACIER BAY NATIONAL PARK

13. ALASKA CHILKAT BALD EAGLE PRESERVE

Description: The preserve, which boasts the world's largest feeding concentration of bald eagles, is one of the best wildlife viewing sites in Alaska. As many as 4,000 bald eagles gather here from late October through February, attracted by rich salmon runs at the silty confluence of the Tsirku and Chilkat Rivers. Biologists estimate that as many as 400 of the magnificent birds make their year-round home in the Chilkat Valley. This area straddles the coastal and interior ecosystems and shares the wildlife of both. Besides eagles, visitors may spot brown and black bears, moose, mountain goats, salmon, river otters, wolves, wolverines, coyotes, and various species of birds, including trumpeter swans and loons. Birders driving into Canada should watch for the shift from chestnut-backed to black-capped chickadees, from Steller's jays to gray jays, and from blue grouse to ruffed and spruce grouse.

Viewing Information: The preserve is accessible by car, with viewing points along the Haines Highway. Rental cars and commercially guided tours are available year-round. SPECTATORS MUST USE DESIGNATED HIGHWAY PULLOUTS AND SHOULD BE CAUTIOUS OF TRAFFIC TRAVELING AT HIGH SPEEDS ALONG THE HIGHWAY. Visitors should also respect the privacy of Klukwan village. For a different perspective, take a guided river trip in the summer. Although there are no visitor facilities in the preserve itself, Haines, less than 20 miles away, offers complete amenities.

Directions: *The main viewing stretch parallels the Chilkat River between mile 18 and mile 24 on the Haines Highway. Haines is accessible by road from Anchorage and other parts of Alaska, Canada, and the U.S. and can be reached by plane, boat, or Alaska Marine Highway System ferry from Juneau.*

Contact: ASP (907) 465-4563

Size: 48,000 acres **Closest Town:** Haines

The peak of the annual gathering of eagles occurs in mid to late November. During this time, as many as 20 of these magnificent birds can be spotted in a single tree.
LON E. LAUBER

14. SUMMIT LAKE/TAWAH CREEK

Description: Summit Lake offers a unique chance to view wetland wildlife species year-round. Trumpeter swans breed, nest, and winter on the lake. Mallards, green-winged teal, northern shovelers, northern pintails, buffleheads, goldeneyes, and mergansers stop and rest here during spring and fall migration. River otters, mink, bald eagles, northern goshawks, and a variety of songbirds inhabit the area. Tawah Creek, which has its source in Summit Lake, is home to salmon. Moose feed on the succulent aquatic vegetation of the Tawah Creek wetlands.

Viewing Information: Watch for sockeye, pink, and coho salmon under the Cannon Beach Bridge between July and November. If you look closely, you may be able to glimpse juvenile salmon not yet ready for life in the ocean. Keep an eye out for black and brown bears.

Directions: Take Cannon Beach Road (about one mile from the airport) or Ophir Creek Road (four miles from the airport). In the winter, these sites are accessible only by snowmobile or cross-country skis.

Contact: USFS (907) 784-3359

Size: 2,000 acres within the 17-million-acre Tongass National Forest

Closest Town: Yakutat

15. SITUK RIVER: NINE MILE BRIDGE

Description: The salmon-rich Situk River meanders through a mosaic of wetlands, shrublands, and forests against the backdrop of the Saint Elias Range. All five species of Pacific salmon spawn in the river, as well as healthy populations of steelhead and Dolly Varden trout. Both brown bears and black bears congregate at the Situk to feed. River otters, mink, and moose are also common. Bald eagles can be seen perching on the high spruce trees waiting for a meal to swim by.

Viewing Information: The best and most accessible place to view salmon along the Situk is Nine Mile Bridge. Between April and November, visitors can count on seeing at least one species of salmon.

Directions: Nine Mile Bridge can be reached via Forest Highway No. 10. From the airport, drive about 4.5 miles on the main road toward Yakutat. The only road intersection is just outside town. Take a right here and drive about nine miles to the bridge.

Contact: USFS (907) 784-3359

Size: 10 acres within the 17-million-acre Tongass National Forest

Closest Town: Yakutat

16. ALASKA MARINE HIGHWAY SYSTEM

Description: Travel the Last Frontier on the "poor man's cruise line." This relatively inexpensive year-round state ferry system connects dozens of Alaska communities in Southeast, Southcentral, and Southwest Alaska. From the decks of large, comfortable ships, visitors observe humpback, gray, and orca whales, Dall and harbor porpoises, sea otters, and Steller sea lions. Harbor seals and cormorants lounge atop the navigation buoys along the route. Use binoculars to see shore-based wildlife: mountain goats, black and brown bears, and Sitka black-tailed deer. Look for bald eagles and gulls overhead, and sea birds, including pigeon guillemots, buffleheads, scoters, harlequin ducks, gulls, and goldeneyes, below. The ship's crew frequently alert passengers to wildlife viewing opportunities.

Viewing Information: Reservations are mandatory for staterooms and private vehicles. Passengers may bring bicycles and kayaks for a nominal fee. Many people sleep on deck or in the warm inside lounges. All vessels offer some sort of food service and shower facilities. The ferry system sponsors natural history lectures, movies, performances by musicians, demonstrations from visual artists, and other activities for passengers, particularly during the summer.

Directions: The eight vessels of the ferry system offer scheduled service to 34 ports on three principal routes. The Southeast system stretches from Bellingham, Washington, and Prince Rupert, British Columbia, to Haines and Skagway; the Southcentral route provides service within Prince William Sound; and the Southwest route ties Homer and Seward to Kodiak and the Aleutian Islands.

Contact: AMHS (800) 642-0066, fax (907) 277-4829.

The M/V LeConte, departing from Juneau, offers stunning views of glaciers along Lynn Canal. Passengers may also spot Steller sea lions on nearby Benjamin Island, seals in Peril Strait, sea otters in Salisbury Sound, and humpback whales in Frederick Sound, Stephens Passage, Icy Strait, and Chatham Strait.
JOHN HYDE

REGION TWO: SOUTHCENTRAL ALASKA

17. Wrangell-St. Elias National Park and Preserve
18. Copper River Delta
19. Alaganik Slough
20. Prince William Sound
21. Portage Valley
22. Windy Corner
23. Beluga Point
24. Glen Alps/Prospect Heights
25. Eagle River Visitor Center
26. Potter Marsh State Game Refuge
27. Eklutna Lake
28. Tony Knowles Coastal Trail
29. Ship Creek
30. Six-Mile Creek
31. Campbell Tract
32. Fort Richardson Army Post
33. Palmer Hay Flats State Game Refuge
34. Sheep Mountain
35. Nancy Lake State Recreation Area
36. Tern Lake
37. Kenai National Wildlife Refuge
38. Kenai River Flats
39. Kenai Fjords National Park
40. Kachemak Bay

Southcentral is Alaska's backyard, its playground. More than half of the state's population lives here: Anchorage is Alaska's largest community. The region offers a taste of all Alaska has to offer. There are sea coasts gilded by the setting sun, alpine peaks outlined in snow, lush forests nibbling at the edges of huge glaciers, rivers and lakes teeming with fish. Most Alaskans believe outdoor recreation, including wildlife viewing, is as critical to their well-being as good nutrition. The variety and excellence of Southcentral's parks, wildlife refuges, trails, and campgrounds reflect the affection Alaskans hold for their land.

FRESHWATER MARSHES: A HAVEN FOR WILDLIFE

The vast wetlands of Alaska provide food and breeding habitat for millions of birds, fish, mammals, amphibians, and insects. At roughly 200 million acres, Alaska's wetlands cover about twice the area occupied by wetlands in the Lower 48 states. Ranging from small ponds,

muskegs, and meadows to forested and tundra wetlands, these areas come alive during spring and summer with the calls of migratory birds. Shown here from top to bottom, left to right: bald eagle, northern harrier, cow moose and calf, trumpeter swan, beaver, Canada goose and goslings, mallard pair, greater yellowlegs, red-necked grebe, muskrat, American wigeon, green-winged teal, and arctic tern.

17. WRANGELL-ST. ELIAS NATIONAL PARK AND PRESERVE

Description: At over 13 million acres, Wrangell-St. Elias is America's largest national park. Nine of the sixteen highest peaks in North America, the continent's largest subpolar icefield, and a glacier bigger than Rhode Island are all found inside its boundaries. Wildlife is plentiful. The mountain ranges are habitat for Dall sheep, mountain goats, and herds of caribou. Moose and brown and black bears share the thick growths of shrubbery and berries in low-lying areas. Bison, transplanted to the area decades ago, roam the Copper and Chitina River valleys. Streams and rivers, splayed in wide deltas, serve as migratory corridors for birds such as lesser yellowlegs, wandering tattlers, mallards, pintails, and green-winged teals. The Copper River drainage and Malaspina forelands are prime nesting sites for trumpeter swans. Steller sea lions, harbor seals, and other marine mammals inhabit the coastline.

Viewing Information: Many nearby communities offer charter aircraft. Regularly scheduled buses take visitors from Anchorage to Valdez and Glennallen during the summer. Backcountry and river guiding services are also available. VISITORS SHOULD RESPECT THE MILLION ACRES THAT ARE PRIVATELY OWNED WITHIN THE PARK.

Directions: *The park has several entrance points. From Valdez, take the Richardson Highway to the Edgerton Highway. From Anchorage, take the Glenn Highway. From Fairbanks, take the Alaska Highway to the Richardson Highway. From Canada, take the Alaska Highway to the Tok turnoff. Follow highway signs.*

Contact: NPS (907) 822-5234; ADF&G (907) 424-3215

Size: 13.2 million acres

Closest Towns: Glennallen, Copper Center, Tok, Yakutat

Dall sheep are high-country dwellers that rest and feed on ridges, steep slopes, and alpine meadows. As rams mature, their horns grow in a circular fashion, reaching a full circle in seven to eight years. A 12-year-old ram is considered very old.
TOM WALKER

Description: The delta's vast wetlands and tideflats are backed by the Chugach Mountains. Each spring, the largest gathering of shorebirds in the western hemisphere stops here on its way to northern nesting grounds. The migrants include nearly the entire populations of western sandpipers and Pacific-coast dunlins, along with thousands of ducks, geese, and swans. Many waterfowl nest in the area, including most of the world's population of dusky Canada geese and more than 7 percent of the world's trumpeter swans. In the spring, brown and black bears come down from the surrounding hills to feed, and the moose bear calves. Weasels, minks, wolverines, river otters, muskrats, beavers, and wolves forage along the beaches and in the aquatic habitats. In the waters off the delta, harbor seals, Steller sea lions, porpoises, and four species of whales feed on the abundant fish and marine life.

Viewing Information: The peak migration period for shorebirds is late April through early May. Hartney Bay, six miles southwest of Cordova, offers excellent viewing of shorebirds, merlins, and peregrines. Dusky Canada geese can be observed along the Copper River Highway from mid-April to mid-October. Trumpeter swans are at Eyak Lake from November through March and along the highway during the spring and summer. Look for bald eagles between mile 27 and mile 37. Don't miss Cordova's annual shorebird festival, held the first weekend in May.

Directions: Take Whitshed Road along the shoreline to Hartney Bay or follow the Copper River Highway 48 miles to its terminus at the Million Dollar Bridge and Childs Glacier. Charter planes provide a good aerial view of the delta and offer access to remote sites.

Contact: USFS (907) 424-7661; ADF&G (907) 424-3215

Size: 700,000 acres

Closest Town: Cordova

Dunlins in breeding plumage descend on the intertidal mudflats of the delta each spring, filling the air with their high, rasping calls. These medium-sized sandpipers nest in the wet tundra of interior Alaska and Canada and winter off the Pacific Coast from British Columbia to the Baja Peninsula. TOM WALKER

SOUTHCENTRAL

3

Description: This 3.2-mile gravel road provides easy access to the wetlands of the Copper River Delta. It meanders through open meadows and around small ponds and sloughs to the edge of Alaganik Slough. A 1,000-foot boardwalk, with interpretive information, viewing blind, and a platform, begins here and leads over the wetlands. Two Forest Service cabins on the delta are accessible from the nearby boat launch.

Viewing Information: In the spring and fall, look for migrating waterfowl and shorebirds, such as the dusky Canada goose, greater yellowlegs, and American wigeon. Bald eagles may circle overhead or perch atop spruce and cottonwood trees. In the summer, watch for breeding trumpeter swans, red-throated loons, horned grebes, pintails, mallards, gadwalls, scaups, and ring-necked ducks in the small ponds that dot the area. Winter visitors may be lucky enough to catch sight of a wolf or moose.

Directions: Alaganik Slough Road is off the Copper River Highway at mile 17, east of Cordova.

Ownership: USFS (907) 424-7661

Size: 17 acres

Closest Town: Cordova

Red-throated loons are one of five loon species found in Alaska. They return every year to the same area to breed. Both parents take turns incubating eggs laid in late May or June. Young often ride on their parents' backs during their first week of life, keeping their soft, downy feathers dry and warm.
ERWIN AND PEGGY BAUER

20. PRINCE WILLIAM SOUND

Description: Some Alaskans insist you can experience the best Alaska has to offer in this single location. The two-million-acre sound includes coastal islands and wetlands, rivers and lakes, muskeg, marshes, forests, and glaciers. Of the wildlife species found in Alaska, a good number can be found here: black and brown bears, mountain goats, Sitka black-tailed deer, moose, harbor seals, sea otters, and thousands upon thousands of marine birds, shorebirds, ducks, songbirds, and raptors. Commonly seen birds include black-legged kittiwakes, parasitic jaegers, black turnstones, surfbirds, yellow-billed loons, puffins, murres, and dunlins. An estimated 3,000 eagles make their home here–the equivalent of the entire eagle population in the Lower 48. The Sound provides critical habitat for Steller sea lions and marbled murrelets, and hosts orcas and gray and humpback whales. Five species of Pacific salmon, Pacific herring, and an abundance of other fish and shellfish provide local communities with a living in commercial fishing.

Viewing Information: A boat affords the best views of wildlife; anything from a luxurious cruise ship to a thin sliver of a kayak will do. Charters are available from most of the sound's larger communities, as well as from Anchorage.

Directions: *Seward, Valdez, Cordova, and Whittier are the main access points for Prince William Sound. Drive to Valdez, fly to the sound from several major cities, arrive by ferry on the Alaska Marine Highway System, or travel by chartered plane, boat, or cruiseship. The Alaska Railroad connects Anchorage to Whittier.*

Contact: USFS (907) 271-2500; Cordova ADF&G (907) 424-3215

Size: 2 million acres   **Closest Towns:** Valdez, Cordova, Seward, Whittier

In 1989, Steller sea lions were designated a threatened species, after their numbers in Alaska declined by 70 percent in about two decades. The causes of the decline are unknown but may include disease, environmental change, and commercial fisheries.
JOHN HYDE/ADF&G

21. PORTAGE VALLEY

Description: At the head of this broad valley, huge icebergs float in 800-foot-deep Portage Lake. Behind the lake, Portage Glacier, a remnant of the Pleistocene Age, slowly recedes. Black and brown bears comb the valley floor and rivers in search of salmon, berries, and vegetation. Mountain goats pick their way along rocky cliffs above timberline. During spring and fall migrations, geese, swans, cranes, and thousands of songbirds pass overhead. Bald eagles nest on the sturdy branches of cottonwood trees. Life is present even within the glacier, where iceworms feed on pollen grains and red algae.

Viewing Information: Look for moose in alder and willow thickets, especially during the winter. Scan the high mountain slopes across from the Begich-Boggs Visitor Center for mountain goats. Check for beavers in Explorer Pond. A viewing platform next to the Williwaw campground provides a bird's-eye view of spawning sockeye, chum, and coho salmon from mid-August through October. Migratory birds fly through from mid-April to late May, and from early August to late September. A viewing deck and boardwalk at mile 1 overlook a 20-acre wetlands area. Forest Service interpreters conduct iceworm "safaris"; check the visitor center for schedules, exhibits, and directions to area trails.

Directions: *Take the Seward Highway south from Anchorage for 45 miles. Turn left on the Portage Highway. The Williwaw fish viewing platform is at mile 4, and the Begich-Boggs Visitor Center is at mile 5.*

Contact: USFS (907) 783-3242

Size: 5,000 acres

Closest Town: Girdwood

Glacier ice is blue because the ice crystals are so dense that few cracks or bubbles are present to reflect light. Only the short blue wavelengths of light are reflected. The blue color is usually more intense on overcast days. WILLIAM GOSSWEILER

22. WINDY CORNER

Description: Visitors heading south from Anchorage on the Seward Highway are treated to grand vistas and the chance to see at least one wildlife species not found in the Lower 48. Dall sheep frequent the steep mountainsides on the north shore of Turnagain Arm each spring and summer. The stocky white sheep—mostly ewes and lambs—come from miles away to eat the mineral-rich soil found here. They often come within several yards of the highway if people don't frighten them away.

Viewing Information: Look for highway pullouts near mile 106; don't park on the highway. Use caution when crossing the road. The best time to view the sheep is midweek, when fewer motorists stop here. DON'T FEED THE SHEEP.

Directions: Windy Corner is at milepost 106 on the Seward Highway, 10 miles south of Potter Marsh.

Contact: ASP (907) 345-5014 or (907) 345-0687

Size: 40 acres

Closest Town: Anchorage

23. BELUGA POINT

Description: Pods of beluga whales pass this rocky point as they chase eulachon and salmon up Turnagain Arm. The 5- to 15-foot whales, small compared to most other cetaceans, breed and bear their young in these silty waters. They are born dark blue-gray, but turn white by age five or six.

Viewing Information: Many points along Turnagain Arm afford views of belugas between mid-April and October. The whales are especially visible on calm days. A large, paved turnout around mile 110.5 has telescopes, interpretative signs, and a spectacular view of the Kenai Mountains. Check the slopes above Beluga Point for Dall sheep, and look for Turnagain Arm's famous bore tide, which can produce a wall of water six feet high roughly an hour after an extremely low tide in Anchorage. DO NOT VENTURE ONTO THE QUICKSAND-LIKE MUDFLATS.

Directions: Beluga Point is at milepost 110.5 on the Seward Highway, 6.5 miles south of Potter Marsh.

Contact: ASP (907) 345-5014; ADF&G (907) 267-2351

Size: 40 acres

Closest Town: Anchorage

24. GLEN ALPS/PROSPECT HEIGHTS

Description: Near these two entrance points to Chugach State Park, spruce woods and mountain hemlock give way to open tundra and jewel-like alpine lakes. From here, visitors can gaze out on the Anchorage Bowl and Cook Inlet. Moose browse on dwarf willow and birch in nearby alpine meadows, and sheep forage in small groups on the mountainsides. Ptarmigan, songbirds, eagles, and snowshoe hares are common sights.

Viewing Information: Hundreds of miles of hiking trails crisscross the park. During the fall, look for groups of moose near the Middle Fork Trail along Campbell Creek. In June and July, wildflowers blanket the area. Scan the south slope of Wolverine Peak for Dall sheep.

Directions: Take the Seward Highway south from Anchorage to O'Malley Road. Turn east toward the mountains. Prospect Heights is at the end of Prospect Drive off Upper O'Malley. To get to Glen Alps from O'Malley Road, take a right on Hillside Drive, a left on Upper Huffman, and veer right on Toilsome Hill Road to the trailhead.

Contact: ASP (907) 345-5014; ADF&G (907) 267-2179

Size: 4,000 acres within the 495,000-acre Chugach State Park

Closest Town: Anchorage

25. EAGLE RIVER VISITOR CENTER

Description: Just 22 miles north of downtown Anchorage, this log cabin visitor center in Chugach State Park is only a step away from the wilderness. The spruce- and cottonwood-filled river valley is surrounded by sheer rock walls. Dall sheep forage on nearby mountainsides, moose and bears amble across trails leading from the visitor center, and beavers fell valley trees to reinforce their lodges.

Viewing Information: Watch for moose when driving along Eagle River Road. In August, red salmon spawn in the river. If their passage is not blocked by beaver dams, look for them from the riverside viewing platform. Take the Rodak Natural Trail (0.6 mile) to see snowshoe hares, spruce grouse, and nesting waterfowl. The Albert Loop Trail (3 miles) features information on the geology of the area. Call for a schedule of walks and talks by volunteer naturalists.

Directions: Take the Glenn Highway north from Anchorage. Exit at Eagle River Loop Road. Cross the bridge to Eagle River and turn right at the first light onto Eagle River Road. Drive 10 miles to the end of the road and the visitors center.

Contact: ASP (907) 694-2108 (summer) or (907) 345-5014

Size: 40 acres within the 495,000-acre Chugach State Park

Closest Town: Eagle River

26. POTTER MARSH

Description: Potter Marsh, at the southern end of the Anchorage Coastal Wildlife Refuge, is one of the most accessible and scenic wildlife viewing areas in Alaska. Spruce, cottonwoods, and alders frame the north and east borders of the marsh. To the south, Turnagain Arm sweeps out to Cook Inlet. Bald eagles, water birds, and spawning salmon flourish here. A 1,550-foot boardwalk with interpretive signs (and, often, local naturalists) provides access to the northern part of the marsh. A small highway pullout at the southern end of the marsh allows for viewing and photography from a vehicle.

Viewing Information: The marsh hosts the greatest number of birds between late April and the end of May. Bald eagles, northern harriers, yellowlegs, Arctic terns, pintails, Canada geese, red-necked grebes, and Pacific loons stay through the summer. Muskrats and moose frequent the marsh year-round; in May and June, look for them in the evenings as they forage on the new green growth. From June through September, three species of salmon return to spawn in Rabbit Creek, which flows under the boardwalk. FISHING IS PROHIBITED. In winter, skiers can follow the tracks of resident snowshoe hares, coyotes, beavers, weasels, mink, voles, and shrews. Ice skaters will find "pushups," piles of sedges stored by muskrats for winter food. Commercially guided tours are available from Anchorage. Visitors should dress for cool, windy weather even on sunny days.

Directions: *The boardwalk starts at the brown highway sign on the Seward Highway at mile 117.4. Drive 10 miles south from downtown Anchorage; the sign is just past the Rabbit Creek Road exit.*

Contact: ADF&G (907) 267-2556; Anchorage bird hotline (907) 338-2473

Size: 540 acres   **Closest Town:** Anchorage

Bird viewing at Potter Marsh is best in the mornings or on those rare days when there is little or no wind. From mid-May through August, numerous species nest and raise young in the marsh, including bald eagles, red-necked grebes, lesser Canada geese, northern shovelers, American wigeons, green-winged teals, yellowlegs, and arctic terns. JOHN SCHOEN

27. EKLUTNA LAKE VALLEY

Description: The retreating Eklutna Glacier carved this valley, creating the basin for Eklutna Lake. Nestled beneath the Chugach Mountains, the seven-mile-long emerald green lake is a haven for canoers, kayakers, anglers, windsurfers, and sailors. Look for moose, muskrats, and waterfowl near the lakeshore. Brown and black bears, wolves, coyotes, and mountain goats live in the wilderness regions of Chugach State Park, and Dall sheep climb the steep hillsides. Smaller mammal inhabitants include fox, lynx, porcupine, hare, ground squirrel, ermine, marmot, vole, and pika. Golden eagles, hawks, ptarmigan, grouse, and several varieties of songbirds nest in the area.

Viewing Information: The trailhead parking area offers interpretive displays and a telescope for viewing wildlife. A rock face at mile 1 of the Lakeside Trail is a spring lambing area and a good place to see Dall sheep year-round. The Twin Peaks Trail (7 miles roundtrip) leads to open alpine tundra, a great view of the lake, and a chance to watch sheep grazing in Goat Mountain Bowl. Take the moderately difficult 6.5-mile East Fork Trail, accessed at mile 10.5 of the Lakeside Trail, to see mountain goats. Both mountain goats and Dall sheep can also be seen from the glacier trail beyond the upper end of Eklutna Lake.

Directions: Take the Glenn Highway northeast from Anchorage to the Eklutna exit (mile 26). Turn right (toward the mountains) and follow park signs 10 miles on a gravel road to Eklutna Lake.

Contact: ASP (907) 688-0908

Size: 50,000 acres within the 495,000-acre Chugach State Park

Closest Town: Eagle River

Mountain goats are one of two species of all-white, hoofed large mammals found in Alaska. They are often confused with young and female Dall sheep but are easily distinguished by their longer hair, deeper chest, and black horns.
TOM WALKER

28. TONY KNOWLES COASTAL TRAIL

Description: A stroll along this spectacular coastal trail is one of the great pleasures of visiting Anchorage. Stretching from downtown Anchorage to the spruce-hardwood forests of Kincaid Park, the 11-mile paved trail offers striking views of Cook Inlet, Mt. Susitna, the Anchorage Coastal Wildlife Refuge, and the Alaska Range, including Mt. McKinley. The trail is popular with cyclists, joggers, cross-country skiers, and wildlife enthusiasts.

Viewing Information: In the summer, watch for such migratory waterbirds as Canada geese, American wigeons, red-necked grebes, and Arctic terns at Westchester Lagoon (mile 1 of the trail). Many birds nest and raise their young here. Further down the trail, look for shorebirds and waterfowl feeding on the mudflats when the tide is out. At Point Woronzof (mile 5), bank swallows dart in and out of their cliffside homes. Watch for bald eagles above and pods of beluga whales pursuing runs of eulachon or salmon below. In the winter, ravens perform their courtship acrobatics here. At Kincaid Park (mile 10.5), visitors have a good chance year-round of encountering moose. During the summer, bald eagle nests may also be sighted. South of Kincaid Park, large flocks of Canada and snow geese gather on the wildlife refuge during spring migration.

Directions: The trail starts at the west end of 2nd Avenue in downtown Anchorage. The many entry points include Westchester Lagoon (near the intersection of 15th and "U" Streets), Point Woronzof (at the west end of Northern Lights Boulevard), and the Kincaid Park outdoor center (at the extreme west end of Raspberry Road).

Contact: MOA (907) 343-4355 and 343-6397 (Kincaid park info)

Size: 11 miles of trail; 1,400 acres of parklands

Closest Town: Anchorage

Alaska Governor Tony Knowles, an avid runner and wildlife watcher, prepares for a jog along the coastal trail. MARK KELLEY

47

29. SHIP CREEK

Description: Ship Creek runs through Anchorage's industrial district, reminding visitors to Alaska's largest city that wilderness is not far away. Throngs of salmon struggle against the creek's current to reach their spawning grounds. A viewing platform within walking distance of downtown hotels provides a good vantage point from which to watch this primordial journey. Next to Elmendorf State Hatchery, two miles upstream, visitors can watch salmon leaping through the air in an attempt to scale an impassable dam. A variety of ducks and geese, including mergansers, mallards, green-winged teal, harlequins, and Canada geese, also frequent the creek and nearby ponds.

Viewing Information: The peak months for watching salmon in Ship Creek are June, July, and August. Look for eagles, beaver, mink, and fox along the creek, and for moose along creekside willow stands near the hatchery.

Directions: To get to the viewing platform from downtown Anchorage, take C Street north to Whitney Road. Turn right and drive 1/2 mile to the parking area on the right across from the power plant. For the Elmendorf State Hatchery, take the Glenn Highway east about 1.5 miles from downtown. Turn left on Reeve Boulevard, then right on Post Road. The parking area is down 300 yards on right.

Contact: MOA (907) 343-4355 (downtown viewing site); ADF&G (907) 274-0065 (hatchery site)

Size: 5 acres

Closest Town: Anchorage

30. SIX-MILE CREEK SALMON VIEWING AREA

Description: Sockeye and pink salmon spawn here and rest while waiting to jump up a fish ladder into Six-Mile Lake. At its peak, between August and mid-September, the creek teems with more than 2,000 fish. Visitors get close-up views from an elevated deck overlooking the creek. During the summer, common loons and red-necked grebes tend their young to the east of the viewing area.

Viewing Information: Obtain a pass at the Elmendorf Air Force Base visitor center before proceeding to the site. Displays at the viewing area describe the life history of salmon.

Directions: Take the Glenn Highway north from downtown Anchorage about 3 miles. Turn left (northwest) on Boniface, travel about 0.5 mile, and stop at the Air Force visitor center for directions to the creek.

Contact: U.S. Air Force (907) 522-2436

Size: 1 acre

Closest Town: Anchorage

31. CAMPBELL TRACT

Description: Within Anchorage city limits, Campbell Tract's four different ecosystems produce a near-perfect representation of the plant, bird, and animal species typical to Southcentral Alaska. Visitors may spot moose and coyotes year-round and black bears in the summer. Two species of salmon spawn here: kings in July and silvers in August and September. The wood frog manages to survive Anchorage's harsh winters, and in the summer, some of Alaska's prettiest wildflowers—fireweed, lupine, monkshood, and larkspur— sprinkle the tract with brilliant color. Bald eagles, great horned owls, spruce grouse, and goshawks are visible year-round. In the spring and summer, the songs of birds like the yellow-rumped and Townsend's warblers and Swainson's and hermit thrushes fill the air. These feathered gypsies have journeyed to Alaska from as far away as Central and South America.

Viewing Information: Trails have been developed for hikers, nature lovers, mountain bikers, equestrians, skiers, and dog mushers. Although the tract itself offers few recreational facilities, the park's location in Anchorage means visitors will have no trouble finding full amenities nearby.

Directions: *Next to Anchorage's Far North Bicentennial Park. The tract has two main Anchorage entrances: one is at the corner of East 68th Avenue and Abbott Loop Road; the other is from Campbell Airstrip Road, 1.1 miles south of Tudor Road.*

Contact: BLM (907) 267-1246

Size: 730 acres. Next to Anchorage's Far North Bicentennial Park.

Closest Town: Anchorage

SOUTHCENTRAL

Fireweed is one of the state's most notable wildflowers. Many residents believe when the last blooms on its tall stalk have fallen that winter is on its way.
JOHN HYDE

32. FORT RICHARDSON ARMY POST

Description: The countless lakes and ponds, extensive forested areas, and tundra-covered mountain slopes of this northern army post help give Anchorage the feel of a city on the edge of wilderness. More than 500 moose roam here; watch them from the post's viewing platform. Visitors can sight brown bears, Dall sheep, and golden eagles from well-marked trails. At Otter Lake, the arrival of common loons and Canada geese heralds summer; beavers and black bears are already up and busy. At Gwen Lake, rainbow trout feed on freshwater shrimp; look also for great horned owls. Further off the beaten track, at Waldon Lake, look for green-winged teal, bufflehead, and American wigeon sliding through the quiet waters. A short distance to the east lies Clunie Lake, habitat shared by common loons and arctic terns. Across the Glenn Highway, Arctic Valley affords spectacular views of Anchorage, Cook Inlet, and Mt. McKinley.

Viewing Information: Obtain a pass and detailed directions to each site at the main gate to the post.

Directions: From downtown Anchorage, take the Glenn Highway 7 miles north to the Fort Richardson exit. At the end of the exit ramp, turn left and cross the bridge. Stay in the right lane; the main gate parking lot is on the righthand side.

Contact: U.S. Army (907) 384-2019 or 384-2072

Size: 62,000 acres

Closest Town: Anchorage

The cry of a common loon piercing the twilight is one of the most thrilling sounds of nature. Loons are an integral part of Alaska's wilderness—a living symbol of its pristine waters. LON E. LAUBER

33. PALMER HAY FLATS STATE GAME REFUGE

Description: North of Anchorage, at the head of Knik Arm, Palmer Hay Flats is a popular waterfowl hunting and viewing area. Tens of thousands of dabbling ducks, primarily pintails, mallards, green-winged teal, and wigeon, and thousands of diving ducks, including canvasbacks, greater scaup, and common goldeneye, arrive on the flats each spring and fall during their annual migration. They are joined by tundra and trumpeter swans, sandhill cranes, and three species of geese: lesser Canada geese, white-fronted geese, and snow geese. The wet meadows and marshes of the refuge are interspersed with islands of spruce trees, and serve as major calving and wintering grounds for the Matanuska Valley moose population. Visitors may also see muskrats, snowshoe hares, red-tailed hawks, and coyotes on the refuge.

Viewing Information: The best time to view migrating waterfowl is between late April and mid-May. Listen for the ancient chorus of the sandhill cranes. Throughout the spring and summer, scan marshes and sloughs at dawn and dusk for muskrats. In mid-July and early August, check for silver salmon in Wasilla and Cottonwood Creeks; bring your fishing rod. In the winter, look for large numbers of moose feeding near the Glenn Highway. REMEMBER: TIDAL MUDS CAN BE TREACHEROUS; TIDAL CHANGES OCCUR RAPIDLY.

Directions: From Anchorage, take the Glenn Highway north to mile 32-34. Rabbit Slough access is at mile 34.7. From Wasilla, take Knik Goose Bay Road 4 miles south to Fairview Loop Road. At mile 1.8, turn on Hayfield Road. Travel 1.2 miles to the Cottonwood Creek access on the left.

Contact: ADF&G (907) 745-5015

Size: 28,800 acres   **Closest Towns**: Wasilla, Palmer

Northern pintails are the most abundant and widely distributed ducks in Alaska. Over a million pintails arrive in Alaska each spring. Referred to as "greyhounds of the air," these sleek and slender ducks have been clocked flying up to 65 miles per hour. MICHAEL DEYOUNG

SOUTHCENTRAL

34. SHEEP MOUNTAIN

Description: Sheep Mountain provides a rare opportunity to watch Dall sheep leaping around in their natural surroundings. Their innate shyness and the remoteness of their alpine habitat make these hoofed acrobats one of the most elusive of Alaska's wildlife species. Sheep are social creatures: one tiny speck of white against the green of a mountain meadow usually means others are nearby. In spring, lambs accompany ewes. Rams challenge each other for dominance at any time of year, and the horn clashing can be heard a mile away. Sheep Mountain sits along a major bird migration corridor; during April, visitors frequently see golden eagles, red-tailed and rough-legged hawks, and other raptors.

Viewing Information: Binoculars are recommended. Visitors often spot sheep on the mountainside right from their cars. In winter, deep snow and spectacular panoramas of the Chugach and Talkeetna Mountains transform Sheep Mountain into a popular recreational area for adventurers on skis, snowshoes, and snow machines.

Directions: Take the Glenn Highway east from Anchorage. The area is on the north side of the road, beginning at mile 107.

Contact: ADF&G (907) 822-3461

Size: 25,600 acres

Closest Towns: Glennallen, Palmer

Dall sheep lambs are born in late May or early June. As lambing approaches, ewes seek solitude and protection from predators in the most rugged cliffs available. Lambs begin feeding on vegetation within a week after birth and are usually weaned by October.

JOHNNY JOHNSON

2

Description: Nancy Lake is one of Alaska's few flat, lake-studded landscapes preserved in its natural state for public recreation and wildlife viewing. Approximately 80 lakes, streams, and swamps lie within its boundaries. The combination of forests, wetlands, and waterways guarantees ideal habitat for beavers, moose, bears, waterfowl, and other birds, such as Arctic tern. Three species of loons—common, Pacific and red-throated—nest here. Each lake has at least one pair of nesting loons, and most are beaver lodge sites. Trout and pike fishing are popular.

Viewing Information: The best way to explore this area is by water. Canoes and kayaks are popular as are the hiking, canoe, and self-guided nature trails. Even novices can complete the eight-mile canoe trail in one long Alaska summer day. The area offers comfortable and convenient public use cabins and campgrounds. Reservations are required for cabin use.

Directions: *From Anchorage, take the Glenn Highway to the Parks Highway. Look for the Nancy Lake Parkway at mile 67.3.*

Contact: ASP (907) 745-3975

Size: 22,685 acres   **Closest Town:** Willow

SOUTHCENTRAL

The beaver is designed to swim and work underwater. Its nose and ear valves close when the beaver is submerged; its broad tail functions like a rudder; and its lips close tightly behind its protruding front teeth, enabling it to cut and chew submerged wood without getting water in its mouth. ERWIN AND PEGGY BAUER

Description: Here in the high mountains of the Kenai Peninsula, even the summers taste of winter. Arctic terns (for which the lake is named) share the area with a variety of song and shorebirds such as the northern waterthrush, golden-crowned sparrow, and greater yellowlegs. The cold, clear waters of Tern Lake also feed common loon, mallard, pintail, and Barrow's goldeneye. The birds are joined by beavers, river otters, and muskrats. Dall sheep and mountain goats need their thick, shaggy coats to survive high on the surrounding slopes; bulky layers of fat and months of winter hibernation protect brown and black bears. Bog rosemary, insect-eating sundews, and cottongrass float on mats of vegetation in the lake. Where the forest and lake meet, moose feed on low shrubs, and bald eagles and other raptors build their nests.

Viewing Information: Easy access, beautiful scenery, and the educational opportunities available at the lake's viewing platform all recommend the area. Visitors can handle resin reproductions of the horns of Dall sheep and mountain goats and the antlers of moose, and can study full-sized tracks of moose and black and brown bears. Exhibits explain how the animals grow and use their horns, how the habitat of each animal is important to it, and how to look for and recognize Alaska wildlife at Tern Lake and elsewhere. A salmon viewing platform is located near the day use parking area for the Tern Lake campground.

Directions: *Tern Lake lies at at the junction of the Seward and Sterling Highways (mile 37 of the Seward Highway).*

Contact: USFS (907) 224-3374

Size: 100 acres **Closest Town:** Seward

Arctic terns are the champion migrants of the bird world, flying about 25,000 miles each year between their breeding grounds in Alaska and their wintering grounds in the Antarctic. They are expert fishers, hovering over a spot until they see a fish, then plunging in after it. During courtship, the male performs a ceremonial "fish flight," in which he carries a small fish in his bill and passes low over a female on the ground.

GRANT KLOTZ

Description: The glaciers and mountain peaks in this popular refuge are more than 6,000 feet high. Below, the spruce and birch forests are reflected in hundreds of lakes. Anglers from around the world come here to cast for salmon, trout, and char in the Kenai and Russian Rivers, sometimes competing with grizzly bears. In the steep, rugged terrain of the Kenai Mountains, Dall sheep forage for low-growing alpine plants. Black bears usually stick to the privacy of forested areas, but may emerge to search for berries in sunlit meadows. In the lowlands, long-legged moose weighing up to 1,600 pounds strip leaves and twigs from willow and aspen trees.

Viewing Information: Look for Dall sheep on mountainsides in the Cooper Landing area (especially on Round Mountain) and along the Sterling Highway at the eastern refuge boundary. Use binoculars to find moose along the Skilak Lake Loop Road, at the Engineer Lake overlook, and near Hidden Creek. Black bears can sometimes be seen in forested areas along the Swanson River and Swan Lake Roads in the northern part of the refuge. In June and July, watch salmon jump the falls along the Russian Lakes trail. Bald eagles are numerous along the Kenai River in winter. Check for trumpeter swans, loons, and mergansers on refuge lakes, especially Hidden, Petersen, Kelly, and Watson Lakes.

Directions: Take the Seward Highway south from Anchorage. At Tern Lake, turn west onto the Sterling Highway. Total trip is 110 miles. The refuge can be accessed from many points along the highway.

Contact: USFWS (907) 262-7021

Size: 2 million acres

Closest Town: Soldotna

Travelers to the Kenai National Wildlife Refuge are treated to panoramic views as they pass through narrow valleys and along turquoise-colored lakes and rivers. The Kenaitze Indians were the first people to inhabit the scenic lake area of the refuge

JOHN HYDE

Description: Each April, the tidal marshes of the Kenai River—still straw-colored from winter dormancy—waken to the energetic honking of snow geese. Huge flocks of the large white birds stop here to feed as they make their way to nesting grounds in Siberia. Caribou bear and rear their young in the wetlands next to the river. Eulachon (a small oily fish) draw harbor seals and beluga whales into the river's mouth, as do salmon in the summer and fall. Two bald eagle nests are located within several miles of the river's mouth.

Viewing Information: As many as 5,000 snow geese may be seen in one day at the peak of their migration, April 17 to 21. Most caribou calve in mid-May, though early May and June witness some calving activity. Other waterfowl and waterbirds that use the flats include northern pintails, mallards, American wigeons, Canada and white-fronted geese, sandhill cranes, and red-throated loons. Many people view birds and other wildlife from pullouts on the Kenai River Access Road near the Warren Ames Bridge.

Directions: From the town of Kenai, take the Bridge Access Road to Kalifornsky Beach Road.

Contact: ADF&G (907) 262-9368; ASP (970) 262-5581

Size: 3,000 acres

Closest Town: Kenai

After leaving the Kenai River Flats, snow geese head to Wrangel Island off Siberia, where they nest. In the fall, some cross the ocean from the Alaska Peninsula back to California. Others take the longer coastal route and winter in Washington or British Columbia. MICHAEL S. SAMPLE

Description: Glaciers have gouged deep fjords into the Kenai Mountains within this national park. Inland, there are broad mountain valleys ringed by wildflowers, a monumental icefield, and jagged peaks. The park is home to some of Alaska's hardiest creatures: moose, mountain goats, black bears, wolverines, and marmots. Sea otters feed in the icy waters in summer. June and July bring humpback whales; watch for orcas in July and August. Look also for gray and minke whales and Dall porpoises. Steller sea lions haul out on islands at the entrances to Aialik and Nuka Bays. Along the sheer cliffs of the Chiswell Islands, the air is raucous with thousands of seabirds, including black-legged kittiwakes, marbled murrelets, common murres, horned and tufted puffins, and rhinoceros auklets. Watch for Peale's peregrine falcons swooping down to grab one.

Viewing Information: Exit Glacier is an ideal open-air classroom for lessons in geology and glaciology. The park offers interpretive exhibits and summertime guided tours. Mountain goats are visible year-round from the glacier and the ranger station. The peak viewing period for bird life is from late May to late August. Take a boat tour of the Kenai Fjords for one of the most spectacular wildlife viewing opportunities in Alaska.

Directions: Bus, train, and air service is available from Anchorage. The ferry connects Seward with Homer, Seldovia, and Kodiak. The Alaska Railroad provides service in the summer. Exploring the fjords by water is popular, but the SEAS CAN BE ROUGH AND DANGEROUS; ONLY EXPERIENCED BOATERS SHOULD ATTEMPT THIS. Commercially guided boats and planes are available.

Contact: NPS (907) 224-3175

Size: 650,000 acres

Closest Town: Seward

SOUTHCENTRAL

The seaward ends of the Kenai Mountains are slipping into the sea, being dragged under by the collision of two tectonic plates of the earth's crust. What were once alpine valleys filled with glacier ice are now deepwater fjords. K.R. WHITTEN

40. KACHEMAK BAY

Description: Spectacular Kachemak Bay is one of the richest marine environments in the world and one of the most popular recreational areas in Alaska. Homer Spit, a sandy shoestring of land jutting 4.5 miles out into the bay, is an excellent spot for watching bald eagles fish waters rich in salmon, herring, and halibut, and for catching a glimpse of sea otters, harbor seals, Dall porpoises, eider ducks, and orcas. Kachemak Bay State Park and the Kachemak Bay State Critical Habitat Area are home to black bears, moose, wolves, mountain goats, and coyotes. Gull Island, located near the park, is a rookery for black-legged kittiwakes, red-faced cormorants, common murres, and the tufted and horned puffins, whose comic antics have earned them reputations as clowns of the bird world. At the head of the bay, Fox River Flats Critical Habitat Area comprises a broad expanse of low-lying marshland and intertidal mud flats, supporting a healthy moose and bear population, as well as an occasional lynx, wolf, and wolverine. Thousands of migrating waterfowl and millions of shorebirds pause along the mud flats each year.

Viewing Information: Good bird viewing opportunities occur in the winter, but wildlife is particularly abundant during the mild summer months. Moose and bear are most plentiful during the spring and fall months. Spring waterfowl migration begins in mid-March; shorebirds begin crowding the coastline in late-April. On the first weekend in May, the town of Homer hosts a shorebird festival that features guided birding tours, lectures, art exhibits, and children's activities. Take the opportunity to view thousands of western sandpipers, surfbirds, and black turnstones. Visitors may want to stop by the newly-constructed wildlife viewing platform across from the Homer Airport terminal. The many charter companies in Homer provide visitors with air, land, and water travel services.

Directions: *Homer can be reached by car via the Sterling Highway, by commercial and charter aircraft, and by ferry boat. Kachemak Bay State Park and its critical habitat area are accessible by boat and plane; access to the Fox River Flats is via a primitive, steep switchback trail from East End Road to the bay.*

Contact: ADF&G (907) 235-7024; Homer Bird Hotline (907) 235-7337

Size: Nearly 400,000 acres

Closest Town: Homer

REGION THREE:
INTERIOR ALASKA

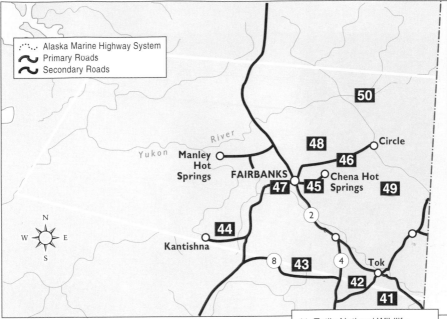

Alaska holds the Interior region close to her heart, this classic Jack London country of log cabins, dog sleds, and northern lights. Spectacular mountain ranges, magnificent rolling rivers, and vast woodlands of spruce and birch trees are habitat for moose, bears, wolves, and Dall sheep. Summer's heat and the frenzied vitality of its wildlife make amends for the pitiless cold that silences this winterfast land during the darkest months. Although landlocked, the mountains of the Interior are colored like orcas, lending the land motion, an impression that helps convey the enormous passage of the land through the seasons.

41. Tetlin National Wildlife Refuge
42. Delta Junction State Bison Range
43. Denali Highway
44. Denali National Park and Preserve
45. Chena River State Recreation Area
46. Pinnell Mountain Recreation Trail
47. Creamer's Field Migratory Waterfowl Refuge
48. White Mountains National Recreation Area
49. Yukon-Charley Rivers National Preserve
50. Yukon Flats National Wildlife Refuge

THE BOREAL FOREST: WOODLANDS OF THE NORTH

Glacier-carved mountains stand sentry over exposed tundra, meandering brooks, and lowlands darkened by spruce and birch trees in the foothills of the Alaska Range. These high-latitude woodlands provide habitat for an abundance of Alaska wildlife. Underlain by frozen ground and located at the northern edge of the treeline, these

forests are adapted to long, cold winters, brief summers, and little precipitation. Trees only inches in diameter may be hundreds of years old. Shown here from top to bottom, left to right: spruce grouse, black-backed woodpecker, raven, Swainson's thrush, gray jay, black bear, boreal chickadee, bull moose, red squirrel, red fox, lynx, marten, and snowshoe hare.

Description: The glacial Nabesna and Chisana Rivers merge to form the mighty Tanana River within the Tetlin National Wildlife Refuge. These expansive flat river basins lead to the foothills of the Nutzotin and Mentasta Mountains, providing a broad range of wildlife habitat. In the spring and fall, the refuge comes alive with the calls of migrating birds, among them sandhill cranes, trumpeter and tundra swans, and white-fronted and Canada geese. The area has one of the highest densities of nesting waterfowl in Alaska; sometimes as many as 65,000 ducklings fledge from these lakes. Visitors may also see Pacific loons, horned grebes, yellow-rumped warblers, and common snipe. During the winter, caribou wander near the highway. Black and grizzly bears, moose, muskrats, and wolves reside within the refuge borders.

Viewing Information: The best time to see sandhill cranes is in mid-September; look for trumpeter and tundra swans in early October. June and July are the peak months for spotted sandpipers and lesser yellowlegs. Lakeview and Deadman Lake offer camping sites. Deadman Lake also features a nature trail, an observation deck, and a fishing pier. Beginning at Midway Lake, seven pullouts along the highway each have an interpretive display. Two fly-in cabins on lakes may be rented. The refuge provides a diverse environmental education program, including a variety of natural history exhibits at the visitors center.

Directions: The Alaska Highway marks the northern boundary of the refuge. Access for small boats is available at Desper Creek and the Chisana River bridge; Deadman Lake has a boat ramp. Floatplanes are available for charter in Tok.

Contact: USFWS (907) 883-5312

Size: 730,000 acres **Closest Town:** Northway

Greater white-fronted geese are distinguishable from other dark geese in Alaska by their pink bills, orange legs, and three-note laughing call. They are among the first waterfowl to arrive in the spring and generally leave by the third week of September. Parents and young form strong family units that remain together until the following breeding season. K.R. WHITTEN

ALYESKA RESORT

1. Attach wire
   wicket to
   ski jacket.

2. Remove
backing. Press
halves together
on wire wicket.

3. Please, throw
   waste in trash.

4. Have a safe
   day skiing.

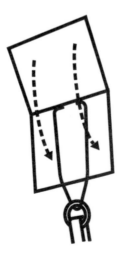

Description: Wood bison became extinct in Alaska about 500 years ago, probably due to changing climate. Plains bison were introduced to the state in 1928. The large shaggy animals, long a romantic symbol of the early American West, have thrived in this area. The permit hunt implemented in 1950 is extremely popular since this herd is one of the few in the world of wild, free-ranging bison. With the development of agriculture in the area in the 1950s, conflicts arose when the 1,000-pound bison began wandering into local farmers' fields, damaging crops. The Delta Junction State Bison Range was established in 1979 to attract the approximately 400 wild bison to managed habitat, away from nearby agricultural lands during crucial growing and harvesting months. Although bison are the most compelling species in the Delta area, wildlife watchers may also see moose, black bears, coyotes, waterfowl, grouse, and other birds.

Viewing Information: Because wildlife viewing is not the main purpose of the range, access may occasionally be restricted and viewing must always be nondisruptive. During the spring and summer, motorists driving the Richardson Highway from Delta Junction to the Black Rapids Glacier may spot bison along the Delta River. The best viewing on the bison range itself is from mid-July to mid-September. Binoculars are helpful.

Directions: The bison range starts about 12 miles southeast of Delta Junction on the Richardson Highway.

Contact: ADF&G (907) 895-4484

Size: 90,000 acres   **Closest Town:** Delta Junction

INTERIOR

Bison, also known as buffalo, are the largest native land mammals in North America. Bulls are often six feet tall at the shoulder, 10 feet long, and weigh more than a ton. Bison move slowly while feeding and appear to be clumsy, but can be quite fleet of foot. A bison in Delta Junction was observed jumping over a seven-foot fence from a standing position. MICHAEL S. SAMPLE

43. DENALI HIGHWAY

Description: This 133-mile highway offers wide-open vistas of mountains, glaciers, tundra, forests, lakes, and rivers. Visitors may see caribou, grizzly bear, and red fox combing the tundra for food while gyrfalcons and long-tailed jaegers circle overhead. Moose, black bears, northern hawk owls, and spruce grouse live in the forests. The many lakes, ponds, and streams near the road provide glimpses of beavers, muskrats, and a variety of birds, including trumpeter swans, loons, oldsquaws, arctic terns, and red-necked phalaropes.

Viewing Information: The highway is generally open from mid-May through September. Posted trailheads on the eastern portion of the road mark good starting points for off-road travel and wildlife viewing. Several canoe routes are also accessible from the highway. Carry extra food, water, and camping equipment as well as a spare tire and jack while driving on this lightly traveled, mostly gravel road.

Directions: The eastern end of the Denali Highway joins the Richardson Highway at Paxson (260 highway miles north of Anchorage; 179 miles south of Fairbanks). Cantwell, at the western end of the Denali, lies on the Parks Highway 210 miles from Anchorage and 148 miles from Fairbanks.

Contact: BLM (907) 822-3217; ADF&G (907) 822-3461

Size: 133 miles

Closest Towns: Paxson, Cantwell

Though this fellow may need a nap, red foxes are generally cunning and intelligent. They are quite vocal and have a large repertoire of howls, barks, and whines. When the hunting is good, red foxes store extra food for leaner times.

JOHNNY JOHNSON

Description: Denali National Park is one of Alaska's premiere sites for wildlife viewing. Beneath dazzling Mount McKinley, North America's highest peak, lies a wide expanse of open tundra, braided rivers and abundant wildlife. Caribou feed on lichen and willows as they migrate along the northern slopes of the Alaska Range. Grizzly bears, often with cubs, dig for ground squirrels and munch on berries. Dall sheep graze high in the alpine tundra, maintaining a safe distance from predators. Visitors often spot moose in the eastern part of the park, and wolves in the more open western part. A variety of species, such as marmots, ground squirrels, red foxes, willow ptarmigan, and spruce grouse, are visible from the park road. Look skyward to catch sight of a long-tailed jaeger, a northern harrier, or a golden eagle.

Viewing Information: Shuttle and tour buses run along a 90-mile gravel road in the park from late May to early September. Bus space is limited; call 800-622-7275 to make reservations or be prepared to wait a day or two. Bring binoculars, warm clothing, raingear, and food. Adventurous travelers should consider a day hike or a backpacking trip in the park. Check for guided ranger hikes and campground talks.

Directions: *Denali lies 240 miles north of Anchorage and 120 miles south of Fairbanks on the Parks Highway. The Alaska Railroad provides daily summer passenger service from both cities. Private vehicles are restricted within park boundaries.*

Contact: NPS (907) 683-2294

Size: 6 million acres

Closest Town Healy

INTERIOR

The grandeur of the Alaska Range is reflected in Wonder Lake, the last stop on the 90-mile bus ride through magnificent Denali National Park. Denali, the name given Mount McKinley by Athabascan Indians, means "The Great One." ALISSA CRANDALL

45. CHENA RIVER STATE RECREATION AREA

Description: Wildlife viewers, anglers, hikers, boaters, campers, skiers, equestrians, hunters, and trappers share this popular recreation area with the moose and the bears. Paddle down the lower part of the Chena River in the summer: the warm air smells of sweet grasses, fireweed, and wild chamomile, and wildlife is visible in its natural setting. Visitors to the area report occasional glimpses of resident wolf packs, and moose wander the sun-speckled woods just off the road. Chena Hot Springs Resort, at the end of the road, is a winter tourist destination.

Viewing Information: Camping is available for a nominal fee. Visitors may stay in public use cabins for a small fee; reservations are required. Chena River has very cold winters; the best time to visit is in the early spring and fall and during the warm, dry summer months.

Directions: *From Fairbanks, take Chena Hot Springs Road east; the recreation area is 26 miles down the road.*

Contact: ASP (907) 451-2695

Size: 254,080 acres

Closest Town: Fairbanks

46. PINNELL MOUNTAIN RECREATION TRAIL

Description: The rugged, 27-mile Pinnell Mountain Trail offers a rich tundra ecosystem a short distance from Fairbanks. Hikers can hear the whistles and squeaks of hoary marmots and pikas alongside the calls of surfbirds. These creatures share the mountainside with caribou, wolves, grizzly bears, and an occasional wolverine. Each spring the alpine tundra hosts migratory birds such as American golden plovers, gyrfalcons, northern wheatears and Lapland longspurs. Rockslide butterflies *Erebia makinlenis* and *Boloria distincta* make their home on the mountain's talus slopes, which sparkle each summer with wildflowers: alpine azaleas, arctic forget-me-nots, mountain avens, and frigid shooting stars, among others.

Viewing Information: The trail is directly accessible from the Steese Highway. Allow at least three days to hike its length.

Directions: *Take the Steese Highway from Fairbanks. The trail meets the road at Twelvemile Summit (milepost 85.6) and at Eagle Summit (milepost 107.3).*

Contact: BLM (907) 474-2200 or 800-437-7021

Size: 79 acres

Closest Towns: Central, Fairbanks

47. CREAMER'S FIELD MIGRATORY WATERFOWL REFUGE

Description: Residents of Fairbanks follow the seasons by observing the changing bird life on Creamer's Field. The return of thousands of waterfowl and sandhill cranes to the refuge's farmlands heralds spring. As these early migrants move north, the forest and wetlands fill with the songs of passerines and other breeding birds, nearly 150 species in all. Moose, red foxes, woodchucks, snowshoe hares, red squirrels, and occasionally a lynx share the fields and wilder habitats with the birds.

Viewing Information: The original farmhouse, nestled in the fields with other historic farm buildings, has been converted to a visitors center with educational displays and a knowledgeable staff of volunteers. Staff lead scheduled nature walks, and self-guided nature trails with interpretive signs traverse the boreal forest and wetlands. The refuge is active year-round. Spring is the most exciting season: geese, ducks, and sandhill cranes pause here on their northern migration, and bald eagles and peregrine falcons hunt in the area. Canada and white-fronted geese, American wigeon, northern pintails, mallards, and other migratory birds use the fields as a staging area in April and May. In the summer, visitors commonly spot red-necked and horned grebes, red-tailed hawks, olive-sided flycatchers, northern waterthrushes, and gray jays. Migrating birds stop at Creamer's again in the fall, on their way south to their wintering grounds.

Directions: Creamer's Field is two miles from downtown Fairbanks. Reach the fields, trails, and visitors center from College Road, and remote sections of the refuge from Farmer's Loop Road.

Contact: ADF&G (907) 459-7213, visitors center (907) 459-7213.

Size: 1,800 acres.

Closest Town: Fairbanks

Creamer's Field, the Fairbanks farm that once provided Gold Rush miners with dairy products almost as valuable as the gold dust they sought, has been converted into a state waterfowl refuge and natural history museum. K.R. WHITTEN

INTERIOR

Description: This remote, rugged area offers outstanding opportunities for canoeing, hiking, and cross-country skiing. Special geographic features include subarctic caves and disappearing streams in the Limestone Jags area; and rocky pinnacles, terraces, and solifluction lobes (unusual permafrost features) on Mt. Prindle. In the summer, visitors may float Beaver Creek, a nationally designated wild river. Wildlife within the area is dispersed. Dall sheep travel in bands around Mt. Prindle and the White Mountains; black bears linger in blueberry thickets in late summer; caribou meander across the tundra and along high ridges, subsisting on lichens and other low-lying plants. Brown bears, moose, wolves, and wolverines also inhabit this largely untouched expanse.

Viewing Information: Look for marmots on rock outcroppings above 3,500 feet and for pikas on scree and rock slopes. Rafters on Beaver Creek may see gyrfalcons near the Limestone Jags, peregrine falcons along bluffs, and bald eagles in treetops at the river's edge. Also keep an eye out for merlins, kestrels, rough-legged hawks, and red-tailed hawks. During the winter, listen for the hoots and cries of hawk owls, boreal owls, great-horned owls, and great gray owls. Watch for caribou when hiking near Mt. Prindle. Trails used primarily in the winter, by dog mushers, snowmobilers, and skiers connect nine public use cabins.

Directions: Take the Steese Highway north from Fairbanks. Turn north on U.S. Creek Road at mile 57. Or, take the Elliot Highway at mile 10 of the Steese Highway just past Fox. Park at mile 28 for the Summit Trail or at mile 57 for the Colorado Creek Trail (not a good summer trail).

Contact: BLM (907) 474-2200 or 800-437-7021.

Size: 1.1 million acres

Closest Town: Fairbanks

Male and female collared pikas live separately for most of the year, marking their territory by rubbing cheek glands against rocks. In the summer and early fall, they gather vegetation, which they leave in the sun to cure like hay: food for the winter.
TOM WALKER

Description: Historic relics, expansive scenery, magnificent summer skyscapes, and abundant wildlife lure adventuresome travelers to this remote preserve. River floaters can see endangered peregrine falcons diving from cliffs at speeds of more than one hundred miles per hour to catch their prey in mid-air. Moose, hidden from their predators in dense brush, bear their calves by the river's edge; and bands of Dall sheep ewes and lambs forage along the bluffs of the Charley River. The mighty Yukon flows through this ancient landscape, supplying the region's inhabitants with king and chum salmon. Nearby, in the historic communities of Circle and Eagle, the style of life and weathered buildings recall Athabascan Indian history, Gold Rush days, the riverboat era, and Alaska's frontier spirit.

Viewing Information: The most popular way to visit the preserve is to float down the Yukon River, taking side trips up major tributary rivers (the Nation, the Kandik, and the Charley) and day hikes in bordering highlands. Look for peregrine falcons along rivers and atop rocky bluffs; forty pairs of these winged hunters nest between Eagle and Circle. Request a list of authorized guides from the National Park Service. WILDERNESS SURVIVAL SKILLS ARE A NECESSITY FOR THOSE VENTURING INTO THE PRESERVE.

Directions: Scheduled air taxis serve Eagle and Circle year-round. These communities can also be reached from the Taylor and Steese Highways respectively. From there, most people boat or float the Yukon River and its tributaries to reach the preserve. Commercial operators also fly into the upper Charlie River.

Contact: NPS (907) 547-2233

Size: 2.5 million acres   **Closest Town**: Eagle

INTERIOR

Peregrine falcons nest along the craggy cliffs of this remote preserve. Prior to 1972, the use of pesticides such as DDT decimated populations of this bird, causing it to be placed on the federal endangered species list. Most populations have now recovered.

TOM J. ULRICH

50. YUKON FLATS NATIONAL WILDLIFE REFUGE

Description: The Yukon River, one of the great rivers of the world, rambles through the heart of this enormous refuge, a wetland basin of more than 40,000 shallow lakes, ponds, and sloughs. The Yukon Flats is internationally celebrated as a cradle for the millions of nesting waterfowl and other migratory birds that converge here each spring. Scaup, pintails, scoters, and wigeons breed here, as do canvasbacks, the "princes of waterfowl." In September, birds gather on the refuge's fertile lakes before taking wing to continue their migratory journeys. The productive wetlands nourish moose, bears, furbearers, and fish, as well as the Athabascan people of the Yukon Flats, who have lived in harmony with the wildlife here for thousands of years.

Viewing Information: Few experiences are more quintessentially Alaskan than paddling the waters of the Yukon River or one of its tributaries. Experienced boaters may canoe, kayak, or raft on their own; others may participate in commercially guided treks. The refuge surrounds several Athabascan villages including Fort Yukon, which has been selected by NASA as a research base for the study of the aurora borealis. Tourists may take a river boat up the Yukon to visit a Native fish camp. When traveling in the refuge, visitors should remember to treat Native properties and people with courtesy and respect.

Directions: Access is primarily by aircraft. There is regular air service from Fairbanks to Native villages; charter and commercial guide services may be obtained in Fairbanks, Fort Yukon, Circle, and at the Yukon River crossing on the James Dalton Highway.

Contact: USFWS (800) 531-0676

Size: 11.1 million acres

Closest Town: Fort Yukon

Millions of waterfowl—including the American wigeon—find the rich grassy waterways of the Yukon Flats area fertile land for breeding and nesting. JOHN HYDE/ADF&G

REGION FOUR:
SOUTHWEST ALASKA

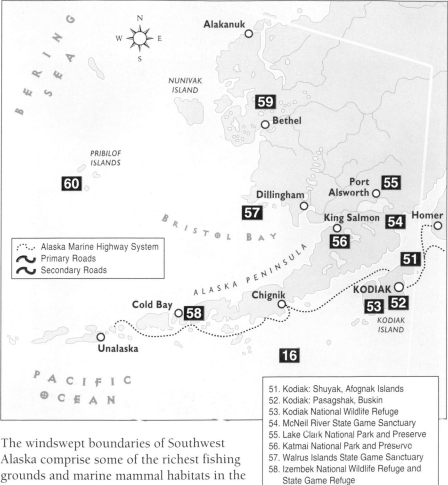

51. Kodiak: Shuyak, Afognak Islands
52. Kodiak: Pasagshak, Buskin
53. Kodiak National Wildlife Refuge
54. McNeil River State Game Sanctuary
55. Lake Clark National Park and Preserve
56. Katmai National Park and Preserve
57. Walrus Islands State Game Sanctuary
58. Izembek National Wildlife Refuge and
    State Game Refuge
59. Yukon Delta National Wildlife Refuge
60. Pribilof Islands

The windswept boundaries of Southwest Alaska comprise some of the richest fishing grounds and marine mammal habitats in the world. Off the rugged Aleutian Islands, blustery waves are whipped into tempests: early Alaskans called the region "Cradle of the Storms." Onshore volcanic and seismic convulsions rearrange the landscape. Enormous brown bears patrol the shorelines bordering the deep, moist forests of Kodiak, Island of Shadows. In the midst of this terrible beauty, whales and walrus trawl the sea and millions of migrating birds darken the sky.

ALASKA'S MARINE ENVIRONMENT: TEEMING WITH LIFE

Alaska's marine environment is rich with fish and wildlife. Shown here from left to right, top to bottom: black-legged kittiwake, Bonaparte's gull, storm petrel, Steller sea lion, double-crested cormorant, horned puffin, common loon, rhinocerous auklet, sea otter, oldsquaw, harbor seal, Dall porpoise, harbor porpoise, Dolly Varden, orca, Pacific herring, salmon shark, salmon, Pacific sand lance, Pacific cod, gray whale, ratfish, China rockfish, skate, and Pacific halibut.

51. KODIAK: SHUYAK ISLAND AND AFOGNAK ISLAND STATE PARKS

Description: Fin, minke, humpback and gray whales, orcas, Steller sea lions, Dall porpoises, harbor seals, and sea otters troll these spruce-clad shorelines. Waters convulsing with screeching, diving birds indicate the presence of whales near shore. Sitka black-tailed deer slip through the dark forests they share with other woodland residents; the haunting cries of the loons herald the first stars. The islands support healthy resident populations of shorebirds and waterfowl, including cormorants, oystercatchers, and marbled murrelets. Jaegers nest on the small islets sprinkled offshore. Afognak Island is also home to herds of transplanted elk.

Viewing Information: In November, look for deer at lower elevations. Watch for tundra swans at the mouths of bays in early April. Humpbacks swim offshore from June through August.

Directions: Afognak and Shuyak Islands lie to the north and east of the city of Kodiak, respectively. They are accessible only by charter boat or floatplane from Kodiak or Homer. Public use cabins can be reserved for a small fee.

Contact: ASP (907) 486-6339

Size: Afognak, 44,000 acres; Shuyak, 11,000 acres   **Closest Town:** Kodiak

52. KODIAK: PASAGSHAK AND BUSKIN RIVER STATE RECREATION SITES

Description: Much of Kodiak Island remains as untamed as when Russians first established a community here in 1792. One of the world's largest islands, it boasts abundant wildlife. In April and again in October, magnificent gray whales migrate through the pass between Narrow Cape and Ugak Island, swimming so close to land that observers can actually hear the chuff of air from their blow holes. Huge Kodiak brown bears lumber across the wind-bludgeoned beaches; herds of semidomesticated bison browse along the green hillsides.

Viewing Information: To watch the gray whales, drive to the end of the road at Narrow Cape and hike up the bluff to the east. Visitors and locals alike enjoy sportfishing and camping at the Buskin River and Pasagshak River State Recreation Sites. Rental cars are available in Kodiak.

Directions: To reach Pasagshak and Buskin, drive south from Kodiak.

Contact: Kodiak Island Convention and Visitors Bureau (907) 486-4782.

Size: Pasagshak State Recreation Site, 20 acres; Buskin River State Recreation Site, 188 acres

Closest Town: Kodiak

Description: Kodiak Island is sometimes called "Alaska's Emerald Isle" for the lush vegetation that blankets its 4,000-foot mountains. Hundreds of miles of coastline, seven major watersheds, and countless lakes, marshes, and meadows are home to abundant wildlife. At least 200 pairs of bald eagles nest on pinnacles, cliffs, and cottonwood trees near the shore. Coastal marshes attract waterfowl and seabirds. Black-legged kittiwakes, horned and tufted puffins, and black oystercatchers nest in shoreline rocks and cliffs. The Kodiak brown bear is the world's largest land carnivore, weighing up to 1,500 pounds and standing sometimes 10 feet tall. From late May to October, these giants feed on the millions of salmon that return to the refuge to spawn. Sitka black-tailed deer, mountain goats, and red fox also live within refuge boundaries.

Viewing Information: The best bear viewing is from mid-June through September near salmon streams, especially Dog Salmon River and Little River. Look for gray whales in Chiniak Bay and Steller sea lions at the downtown dock. Reservations for nine public use cabins are awarded through a quarterly lottery. Guides, outfitters, and lodge operators can assist with wildlife viewing tours.

Directions: Take a 1-hour flight from Anchorage or a 12-hour ferry ride from Seward to Kodiak Island, then charter a small floatplane or boat into the refuge.

Contact: USFWS (907) 487-2600

Size: 1.5 million acres   **Closest Town**: Kodiak

Brown bear cubs are born in January or February in the safety of winter dens. At birth, they weigh less than a pound. They typically stay with their mother until May or June of their third summer. TOM WALKER

54. MCNEIL RIVER STATE GAME SANCTUARY

Description: The largest known gathering of brown bears in the world happens at McNeil River. Visitors get an unparalleled opportunity to watch the bears mating, fighting, playing, and feeding. In early July, chum salmon return to the river to spawn. A series of cascading rapids and pools slows the migration of the salmon and makes them easy prey for hungry bears. More than 100 bruins use the area during the peak of the run in late July. Earlier in the season, red salmon return to adjacent Mikfik Creek, and up to 25 bears are there, plunging into the cold water in pursuit of the darting fish. Visitors may also see harbor seals, moose, red fox, and a great diversity of birds, including cormorants, harlequin ducks, bald eagles, glaucous gulls, and songbirds.

Viewing Information: Apply by March 1 for a permit to visit the popular sanctuary. Permits are awarded through a lottery and are valid for an assigned four-day period between June 7 and August 26. Each day, up to 10 permit holders hike to one of the bear viewing areas, accompanied by an Alaska Department of Fish and Game naturalist. Typically, groups spend six to seven hours watching and photographing the bears. Visitors camp at an established campground and cook in a nearby cabin.

Directions: Although the sanctuary is accessible by boat, virtually all visitors fly from Homer to McNeil using one of several air charter companies.

Contact: ADF&G (907) 267-2180.

Size: 114,200 acres   **Closest Town**: Homer

McNeil River is the world's best wildlife viewing site for the magnificent Alaska brown bear. Usually solitary animals, as many as three dozen bruins may be seen at the river's falls dining on chum salmon. TOM WALKER

Description: The scenery in this park and preserve is unrivalled. Two active volcanoes, Iliamna and Redoubt, rise more than 10,000 feet and vent steam from snow-capped peaks. On the eastern flank of the Chigmit Mountains, rivers cascade to Cook Inlet through forests of Sitka and white spruce. Swans and other waterfowl nest on marshes and outwash plains. Puffins, cormorants, kittiwakes, and other seabirds raise their young in rocky cliffs. Offshore, harbor seals and beluga whales prey on eulachon and other fishes. The western flank of the Chigmits descends through tundra-covered foothills to boreal forest. Lakes and rivers fill the valleys, the water flowing southwestward to Bristol Bay. This region is rich in breeding birds, including golden plovers, wandering tattlers, and surfbirds. Arctic grayling, rainbow trout, Dolly Varden, lake trout, northern pike, and five species of salmon populate the waters. The valleys are home to Dall sheep, caribou, moose, brown and black bears, wolves, lynx, foxes, and other mammals.

Viewing Information: The park offers no developed trails or other public facilities. Visitors may hire a guide. Enjoy a float trip down one of the park's wild rivers or a backpacking trip through the open tundra of the western foothills. Between June and early August, viewers may see up to 30 brown bears along the tidal marshes of Tuxedni and Chitina Bays. In June, harbor seals bear their pups in Tuxedni Bay.

Directions: The park has no highway access. Scheduled flights carry visitors from Anchorage to Iliamna and Port Alsworth. Chartered flights are available from Anchorage, Kenai, or Homer.

Contact: NPS (907) 781-2218

Size: 4 million acres

Closest Town: Anchorage

The long ear tufts of a lynx serve as antennae, enhancing its ability to hear snowshoe hares, the lynx's primary prey. The large, broad feet of the cat function as snowshoes to aid in winter traveling and hunting.
TIM CHRISTIE

Description: The 1912 eruption of Novarupta—ten times more forceful than the eruption of Mount St. Helens and twice as violent as Krakatoa—dramatically transformed the Katmai area. It remains one of the most fascinating geological sites in the world today. On the drive from Brooks Camp to the Valley of Ten Thousand Smokes, visitors may observe 30 to 40 species of birds, as well as bears, moose, and wolves. Brooks Camp offers two brown bear viewing platforms. More than a million red salmon migrate annually from Bristol Bay into the Naknek system of rivers and lakes. The islands along the coast boast marine mammal haulouts and colonies of seabirds; brown bears and eagles gather along snow-fed creeks. Tundra ponds are home to a variety of waterfowl, beavers, and river otters. Katmai hosts many species of birds, including Swainson's thrushes, Wilson's warblers, ospreys, merlins, northern harriers, fox and American tree sparrows, and dark-eyed juncos.

Viewing Information: Brown bears are active from May through October; the best viewing is in July and September. Wolves, moose, and beavers are also most visible during the summer. Red salmon begin migrating in late June and begin spawning in August.

Directions: Daily commercial flights from Anchorage bring visitors to King Salmon, 6 miles from the park and 30 miles from the Brooks Camp brown bear viewing platforms. Charter flights are available from King Salmon year-round. The lodges and the campground require reservations.

Contact: NPS (907) 246-3305

Size: 4.1 million acres

Closest Town: King Salmon

SOUTHWEST

Brooks Camp provides visitors to this park with a rare closeup of the brown bears for which Katmai is famous. ALISSA CRANDALL

Description: These seven small, isolated islands in Bristol Bay host the largest annual land-based walrus haulout in the Western Hemisphere. Each spring, 2,000 to 10,000 male walruses bask on the rocky beaches of Round Island for days at a time. Steller sea lions have a rookery nearby and gray whales swim offshore along the coast. In spring and summer, red foxes feed and play on the island slopes. Hundreds of thousands of seabirds, including kittiwakes, murres, puffins, cormorants, parakeet auklets, and pigeon guillemots, breed along the islands' shores during the summer.

Viewing Information: Viewing, by permit only, is from May 1 to August 15. Five-day permits allowing camping on Round Island may be obtained on a first-come, first-served basis from ADFG in Dillingham. VISITORS MUST BE SELF-SUFFICIENT, IN GOOD PHYSICAL CONDITION, AND PREPARED FOR INCLEMENT WEATHER.

Directions: Jet service runs to Dillingham, and smaller charter planes fly to Twin Hills on Togiak Bay. At Twin Hills, charter a boat to Round Island. Tumultuous seas and gale-force winds are not uncommon, and travel is expensive and weather dependent.

Contact: ADF&G (907) 842-2334
Size: 4,480 acres   **Closest Town:** Dillingham

Social animals, male walruses gather in herds and will lunge to the defense of their neighbors if attacked. They can dive to 300 feet and remain submerged for up to 30 minutes. Males eat up to 100 pounds of food daily but may haul themselves out of the water for a week without feeding.

LON E. LAUBER

58. IZEMBEK NATIONAL WILDLIFE REFUGE AND IZEMBEK STATE GAME REFUGE

Description: Izembek is a major migratory staging area for Pacific brant, emperor geese, and Steller's eiders. Volcanos, snowfields, lakes, and rivers also adorn the refuge. One of the world's most extensive eelgrass beds is visited each autumn by more than a quarter of a million migratory birds. Besides 185 species of birds, the refuge complex is home to 23 species of land and marine mammals and 40 species of fish, including orcas and gray whales, caribou, brown bears, and the world's only nonmigratory population of tundra swans.

Viewing Information: Waterfowl congregate at Izembek Lagoon in September and October. In late October and early November, caribou gather near the road system. Look for orcas in the fall and gray whales in the spring. River and sea otters, harbor seals, wolverines, and red foxes are visible year-round. The peak viewing season for brown bears is in July and August, though they are abundant from June through October. Pick up a copy of the free wildlife viewing guide prepared by the Izembek refuge manager.

Directions: *Take a jet or a ferry boat to Cold Bay. The 40-mile Cold Bay road system offers some refuge access; rent vehicles at Cold Bay. Charter flights provide access to other portions of the complex.*

Contact: USFWS (907) 532-2445 **Size:** 2.9 million acres **Closest Town:** Cold Bay

59. YUKON DELTA NATIONAL WILDLIFE REFUGE

Description: The powerful Yukon and Kuskokwim rivers dominate the refuge, the second largest in the nation. In spring and fall, the broad river deltas and wetlands nurture a massive number of migrating ducks, geese, swans, cranes, and shorebirds. A narrow strip of coastline between Nelson Island and the Ashinuk Mountains is the world's primary nesting habitat for four species of geese: blank brant, emperor, cackling Canada, and Pacific greater white-fronted. Steep cliffs on the southwest coast of Nunivak Island host upwards of one million seabirds. Roughly 500 muskoxen share the rest of Nunivak Island with a commercial herd of reindeer. Moose, caribou, bears, and wolves inhabit the northern hills and eastern mountains.

Viewing Information: Walrus, whales, and seals migrate offshore in spring. Hooper Bay and Chevak are good shorebird viewing spots. Float the Andreafsky River to see wildlife from a different angle. The city of Emmonak offers Lower Yukon River boat tours. Several guides based in Mekoryuk lead excursions on Nunivak Island.

Directions: *Anchorage and Fairbanks offer airline service to Bethel, St. Mary's, and Aniak. All delta villages can be reached from Bethel via daily scheduled and/or charter flights.*

Contact: USFWS (907) 543-3151

Size: 19.6 million acres **Closest Town:** Bethel

SOUTHWEST

60. PRIBILOF ISLANDS

Description: Each summer, nearly a million northern fur seals gather on these remote Bering Sea islands to give birth to their pups. Males weighing 600 pounds or more stand guard over their harems, going without food for up to three months. Millions of sea birds also descend on the rocky island outposts. Rare Asiatic vagrants and other "accidental" species happen by between mid-May and June. Birdwatchers may spot red-faced cormorants, red-legged kittiwakes, northern fulmars, thick-billed murres, horned and tufted puffins, parakeet, least, and crested auklets, and other interesting species nesting in the islands' rugged cliffs and windswept tundra. Visitors may also see arctic blue fox, reindeer, sea lions, and several species of whales. The unique customs of the islands' Aleut inhabitants and the legacy left by 18th century Russian explorers make the Pribilofs a destination of cultural interest as well.

Viewing Information: The best time to visit is between mid-May and August, when a variety of migratory birds and sea mammals are abundant. Fur seal numbers peak in July. Access to their rookeries and haulouts is restricted; visitors must use special observation blinds. AVOID DISTURBING SEALS LEST THEY TRAMPLE PUPS.

Directions: Take a commercial flight to St. Paul or St. George from Anchorage. Inter-island flight service depends on weather. Find out about special tours for birders and other wildlife watchers.

Contact: Tanadgusix Corp. (907) 278-2312; Tanaq Corp. (907) 562-3100; USFWS (907) 235-6546

Size: 51,000 acres

Closest Towns: St. Paul/St. George

More than two-thirds of the world population of northern fur seals breeds here each year. The underfur of these seals is extremely thick at over 300,000 hairs per square inch. Large males arrive first in May and June to establish territories. As many as 100 females eventually gather within each territory. K.R. WHITTEN

REGION FIVE:
FAR NORTH ALASKA

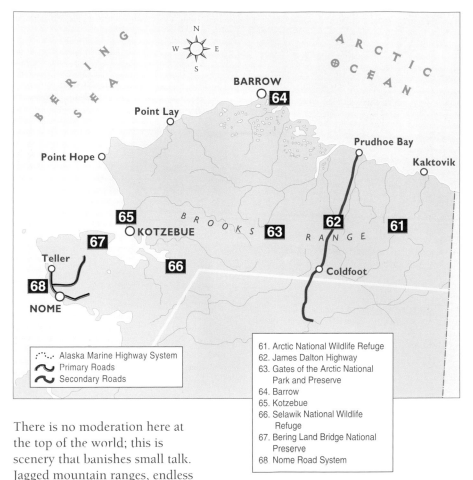

61. Arctic National Wildlife Refuge
62. James Dalton Highway
63. Gates of the Arctic National
    Park and Preserve
64. Barrow
65. Kotzebue
66. Selawik National Wildlife
    Refuge
67. Bering Land Bridge National
    Preserve
68 Nome Road System

There is no moderation here at the top of the world; this is scenery that banishes small talk. Jagged mountain ranges, endless plains of tundra, and broad tumbling rivers give the impression of enormous strength, the grace of brutal power. Spring comes carefully to this land; winter is never far away. Rising bravely from the frozen ground, wildflowers lap up the thin but ever present arctic summer sunshine, their colors crowding and jostling one another across sweeping slopes shared by migrating caribou, solitary brown bears, and companionable herds of muskoxen. Polar bear stalk seal on the ice pack. The geese cry their farewells in the cold distance.

ARCTIC TUNDRA: SUMMER AWAKENING

The frozen north comes alive briefly during Alaska's fleeting summer. Wildflowers, such as purple mountain saxifrage and moss campion, burst through the thin layer of soil; small mammals scramble to replenish their reserves of fat; and great herds

of caribou descend on the windswept coastal plain to bear their young. The environment is fragile, yet tremendously productive. Shown here from top to bottom, left to right: long-tailed jaeger, snow geese, tundra swans, caribou, grizzly bear, muskox, gray wolf, Pacific brant, snow bunting, oldsquaw, arctic fox, snowy owl, American golden plover, and collared lemming.

83

61. ARCTIC NATIONAL WILDLIFE REFUGE

Description: Nature remains essentially undisturbed in this vast, unbroken refuge, the largest national wildlife refuge in the nation. The 150,000-member Porcupine caribou herd calves on the coastal plain from May to mid-June. Bears lumber through alpine meadows, forests, and river bottoms, searching for ground squirrels, carrion, roots, and berries. Visitors to the remote area may see wolves out hunting, Dall sheep feeding on the mountainsides, and muskoxen foraging along river valleys. Snowy owls, jaegers, tundra swans, snow geese, eiders, Lapland longspurs, and many other bird species, nearly 170 in all from several continents, use the refuge.

Viewing Information: River rafting and/or backpacking trips provide excellent opportunities to view wildlife. The refuge offers no designated campsites or marked trails; only highly-skilled wilderness travelers should venture out without a guide. The landscape is fragile, weather can be unpredictable, and mosquitoes can be intolerable.

Directions: The Dalton Highway comes close to a small portion of the refuge's western boundary, but there are no roads to or in the main part of the refuge. Most visitors charter aircraft from Fairbanks, Fort Yukon, Arctic Village, Deadhorse (Prudhoe Bay), or Kaktovik. Planes land on gravel bars, lakes, and tundra sites. Changeable weather frequently delays flights, so take extra food and supplies. Visitors passing through villages should be sensitive to local customs.

Contact: USFWS (907) 456-0250 **Size**: 19.3 million acres

Closest Towns: Kaktovik to the north; Arctic Village to the south

Calving grounds for the Porcupine caribou herd, this refuge is wild and spectacular, even by Alaska standards. Lucky visitors may witness caribou migrations, as thousands of animals sweep across the open tundra to find relief from insects along the arctic coast. TOM WALKER

62. JAMES DALTON HIGHWAY

Description: Driving the gravel James Dalton Highway through the center of the Alaskan wilderness is one of America's great motoring adventures. The scenery is magnificent, from the spectacular peaks of the Brooks Range to the broad sweep of tundra blanketing the coastal plain. The 30-mile stretch between Atigun Pass and Galbraith Lake is one of the finest viewing areas in Alaska for Dall sheep. Galbraith is a lambing area and Atigun is a rearing area for lambs. Motorists may see muskoxen, arctic foxes, and caribou throughout most of the year. In June, when grasses and lichen poke through roadside rinds of half-melted snow, concentrations of geese and other birds such as tundra swans, red-throated loons, and oldsquaws cluster beside the highway. Also, north of the Brooks Range, watch for peregrine falcons, gyrfalcons, rough-legged hawks, Smith's longspurs, bluethroats, and golden eagles.

Viewing Information: The best time to drive the Dalton highway is between late May and mid-September. Ask the BLM for their checklist, "Birds Along the Dalton Highway." Coldfoot, Deadhorse, and the Yukon River bridge are the only places with gas stations, restaurants, and hotels. DRIVERS BEWARE: MORE THAN 100 MILES SEPARATE SERVICES, AND EMERGENCY ROAD ASSISTANCE CAN BE VERY EXPENSIVE. The oil companies that manage Prudhoe Bay must approve access to that area; guided tours are available.

Directions: *Drive north out of Fairbanks on the Steese Highway; at Fox, take the Elliott Highway 74 miles north to Livengood. The Dalton Highway begins a few miles north of Livengood.*

Contact: BLM (907) 474-2320 or 800-437-7021

Size: 414 miles   **Closest Towns:** Fairbanks, Coldfoot

FAR NORTH

Marmots are always alert for predators, including eagles, foxes, coyotes, wolves, and bears. They are sometimes difficult to spot as the color of their pelts blends well with the lichen-colored rocks and rusty-brown soil of their surroundings. True hibernators, marmots spend two-thirds of each year in their winter dens. JOHNNY JOHNSON

63. GATES OF THE ARCTIC NATIONAL PARK AND PRESERVE

Description: Forested southern foothills rise to limestone and granite peaks more than 7,000 feet high in this remote wilderness park. North of the peaks, clear water rivers run through glacier-carved valleys; and tundra, covered with wildflowers during the brief northern summer, stretches toward the Arctic Ocean. Many of the 450,000 caribou of the Western Arctic herd migrate through the park each fall. Brown and black bear, wolf, Dall sheep, lynx, moose, wolverine, and red fox live here year-round. In the spring, the park hosts migratory birds from Europe, South America, Asia, tropical archipelagos, and the continental U.S.

Viewing Information: Backpacking and river trips maximize your chances of encountering wildlife. In late July and August, look for caribou in the Noatak and Killik River drainages. Dall sheep forage on the mountainsides in northern and western areas of the park. Falcons, rough-legged hawks, and golden eagles nest on cliff faces along river valleys. From late August to mid-September, watch for flocks of snow and Canada geese flying south over the Kobuk River. The park offers no facilities; visitors must be skilled in wilderness survival. The park staff can provide a list of licensed guides, outfitters, and air-taxi operators.

Directions: Commercial planes fly from Fairbanks to Bettles, Anaktuvuk Pass, or Coldfoot. Charter a small plane to a trip starting point. Or, drive the Dalton Highway to Coldfoot or Wiseman and hike into the park.

Contact: NPS (907) 456-0281

Size: 8.4 million acres

Closest Towns: Fairbanks, Bettles, Coldfoot

Winter comes early in the north country. Here the photographer has caught the first snow of the season—in August—in the Arrigetch Peaks region of this national park.
MICHAEL DEYOUNG

64. BARROW

Description: America's northernmost city and Alaska's largest Inupiat Eskimo village, Barrow is encircled by ice and snow for nine months of the year. Spring arrives with an explosion of life: millions of birds and thousands of bowhead and beluga whales migrate through the area. Ringed and bearded seals, walrus, and other marine mammals swim the sea; caribou and foxes roam the land. The Inupiat call the area around Barrow "Ukpeagvik," which means "the place of the snowy owl." Great numbers of these huge, silent birds feed and nest here when food is plentiful. The area is also one of the few known nesting spots for Steller's and spectacled eiders. The passage of Ross' gulls from Siberia in late fall heralds the return of snow and ice.

Viewing Information: The road system provides the majority of viewing opportunities. Point Barrow, a spit of land northeast of town, is an excellent area for observing seabirds such as glaucous, Sabine, and ivory gulls, black guillemots, shearwaters, and murres.

Directions: Barrow is served by commercial jet from Anchorage or Fairbanks.

Contact: Barrow municipal offices (907) 852-2511

Size: 19,200 acres

Closest Town: Barrow

65. KOTZEBUE

Description: Kotzebue is Alaska's second largest Inupiat Eskimo village. Anchored to Alaska's northwest coast, it offers excellent opportunities for viewing some of the arctic's most interesting species of birds. Kotzebue also provides a portrait of the lives of Alaska Natives and of the economic and cultural importance of wildlife to the state's indigenous peoples.

Viewing Information: Wonderful birding opportunities exist during spring migration, especially from mid-May through mid-June. The area offers an intriguing juxtaposition of brackish wetlands, lagoons, moist upland tundra, and thickets of willow and alder. Ducks, geese, shorebirds, songbirds, and jaegers are abundant. Birders may also enjoy observing tundra swan, sandhill cranes, short-eared owls, and Alaska's state bird, the willow ptarmigan.

Directions: View wildlife from roadways throughout town.

Contact: Kotzebue Municipal offices (907) 442-3401

Size: About 16,000 acres **Closest Town:** Kotzebue

FAR NORTH

Description: The estuaries, river deltas, and tundra hills of this refuge straddle the Arctic Circle. The Waring Mountains lie to the north of the refuge, the Continental Divide between the Arctic and Pacific Oceans is at its southeastern border, and the Selawik River flows through its center. Largely wetland, the refuge nurtures over 180 species and subspecies of birds, including willow ptarmigans, Pacific loons, arctic terns, and alder flycatchers. The expanse of open tundra is a splendid backdrop to the spring migration of caribou and the autumn mating rituals of moose. Wolf packs lope across the grasses in search of prey; black and brown bears forage the stunted shrubbery for sweet berries.

Viewing Information: Journey down the upper reaches of the Selawik River for the best view of the area's wildlife. The Selawik is a designated national wild and scenic river.

Directions: *The refuge is accessible by charter boat and plane from Kotzebue, Kiana, Noorvik, Selawik, and Ambler. In the winter, visitors may also travel by snowmachine, dog sled, and skis. The Inupiat villages of Noorvik and Selawik lie within the refuge itself, but Kotzebue is the closest community with a range of services.*

Contact: USFWS (907) 442-3799 or 800-492-8848; ADFG (907) 442-3420

Size: 2.15 million acres.   **Closest Town:** Kotzebue

A plump willow ptarmigan, Alaska's state bird, is camouflaged in its winter plumage from predators here along the Arctic Circle. The wetlands of the Selawik Refuge attract diverse species of birds. K.R. WHITTEN

Description: The Bering Land Bridge Preserve is one of America's most remote and least-visited national parks. Reindeer, muskoxen, moose, and polar bears roam across the stark primeval landscape. Bowhead and beluga whales and walrus swim just offshore. In the summer, a storm of migrating birds darkens the sky. The preserve offers excellent viewing of plovers, jaegers, and gyrfalcons. Thousands of years ago, earth and ice may have bridged the 55 miles between Alaska and Siberia, allowing people and animals to cross into North America from Asia; the present-day preserve contains prehistoric sites of early humans, as well as geologic remnants of ancient volcanic activity. Visitors to the Inupiat Eskimo villages near the preserve have an opportunity to learn about Native subsistence, reindeer herding, and the relationship between Alaska's indigenous peoples and its wildlife.

Viewing Information: Visit the Serpentine Hot Springs, where granite spires called "tors" stand guard over steaming pools. A public use cabin that sleeps 20 is next to the natural springs; reservations are recommended. The weather can be harsh even in the summer; visitors should come prepared for dramatically changing conditions. THE ISOLATION HERE DEMANDS SELF-RELIANCE.

Directions: *Commercial jets serve Nome and Kotzebue. In summer, charter a boat or plane into the preserve; in winter, rent snowmachines, dog sleds, or ski planes.*

Contact: NPS (907) 443-2522

Size: 2.7 million acres   **Closest Town:** Nome

Powerful and patient predators on land, ice, and sea, polar bears sniff out breathing holes gnawed in the ice by seals. When a seal finally surfaces, the bear uses his huge claws and teeth to grab his prey and draw it onto the ice.
JOHNNY JOHNSON

FAR NORTH

Description: Three main gravel roads and a handful of smaller roads comprise the Nome road system, a 200-mile invitation to explore the unique Seward Peninsula. Looking east from the Nome-Council Road, visitors may spot beluga and gray whales, harbor porpoises, and seals. Slicing deep into the Seward Peninsula, the Kougarok Road is surrounded by vast homelands to red fox, moose, Arctic ground squirrels, grizzly bears, and raptors such as rough-legged hawks, gyrfalcons, and northern harriers. Muskoxen and reindeer browse along the road system; the Kougarok Road offers views of a resident herd of muskoxen. A private, working reindeer corral is at the road's 12.5-mile mark; visitors may see a reindeer roundup in progress. The open tundra of the peninsula and its proximity to Siberia make this a birdwatcher's paradise, with the chance to see bluethroats, Eurasian wigeons, and other species rarely observed on the North American continent. When spring reclaims Safety Sound, tundra swans, Canada geese, and arctic terns arrive by the thousands. On the Nome-Teller Road there are nesting long-tailed jaegers, golden plovers, whimbrels, and even Old World migrants such as arctic warblers.

Viewing Information: Roads are gravel and can be rough. Beware of inclement weather and biting insects. Rental cars and guide services are available; Nome is the only place to find services and gasoline.

Directions: *Jets fly to Nome from Anchorage.*

Contact: Nome City Visitor Center (907) 443-5535; ADF&G (907) 443-2271

Size: More than 200 miles   **Closest Town:** Nome

When threatened, a herd of muskoxen forms a fortress-like ring with young or injured animals inside. Muskoxen underwool—called qiviut by Alaska Natives—is considered the warmest wool in the world. ERWIN AND PEGGY BAUER

SEASONAL WILDLIFE CALENDAR

Spring: March, April, May

In March, ptarmigan migrate to central Alaska river valleys. Millions of water-fowl and shorebirds return to the Stikine River Flats, Copper River Delta, and other wetlands in April. As spring progresses, the migration north intensifies. Bears begin to emerge from dens. Mountain goats and Dall sheep move to lower elevations, and caribou begin migrating toward calving areas. In May, migratory songbirds begin to arrive, and seabirds appear at southcentral nesting colonies. Steller sea lions begin to gather at coastal rookeries. Walrus and bearded and ringed seals are visible along the western coastline. Gray whales pass through the Gulf of Alaska. In late spring, wolves, caribou, moose, muskoxen, Dall sheep and goats bear their young.

Summer: June, July, August

Dall sheep congregate at mineral licks in late June. Deer fawns are born. June is the best month to spot unusual birds such as Asian accidentals in western Alaska and to look for nesting sandhill cranes. July is the best month to visit seabird colonies from Southeast to Northwest Alaska. Fur seal pups are born on the Pribilof Islands; Steller sea lions bear their young in coastal rookeries. Pacific salmon begin entering fresh water in June; most spawning takes place from July through November. Bears frequent salmon streams and berry patches. Caribou form spectacular aggregations on arctic and alpine tundra. In July, walruses haul out on Round, Little Diomede, and King islands. July is also the best month to observe humpback whales. Starting in July, muskoxen begin their rut. In late summer, the southward migration begins for waterfowl, shorebirds, and songbirds.

Autumn: September, October

September is the peak of waterfowl and sandhill crane southward migration. Harbor seals haul out on Gulf of Alaska coasts. Gray, bowhead, and beluga whales migrate along the west coast. In September, moose and caribou begin to rut. In October, ivory gulls appear near Point Barrow; brant, emperor geese, and Steller's eiders congregate at Izembek Lagoon. Ptarmigan also form large flocks in subalpine areas. Hares, arctic fox, ptarmigan, and lemmings turn white. Caribou migrate to their winter ranges.

Winter: November, December, January, February

In November, thousands of bald eagles congregate along the Chilkat River near Haines. Dall sheep, deer, and mountain goats are in the peak of the rut. As snow deepens, goats move to old-growth forests, Dall sheep to windblown ridges, and deer to beaches. The tracks of furbearers like wolves, wolverines, lynx, marten, and foxes can be seen in the snow. In January, the world's population of emperor geese gathers along Aleutian Island coasts. In February, owls begin singing to stake out breeding territories. Ice-free coastal waters harbor a surprising variety of waterbirds.

BIRDING IN ALASKA

Four hundred and forty-three bird species have been reported in Alaska. The state offers extraordinary opportunities to observe birds unique in North America and even the world. Spotting such species can be the thrill of a lifetime for bird watchers.

Some species breed only in Alaska and are not found elsewhere in North America. These include the red-faced cormorant, the red-legged kittiwake, several species of auklets, and the bristle-thighed curlew. The curlew, which nests only in western Alaska and winters in the South Pacific, lays its eggs in a depression in the tundra or on flat, dry, exposed ridges. The first nest of this little-known bird was discovered on the lower Yukon River in June 1948.

Some birds may nest in other parts of the world, but in North America, only do so in Alaska or Northwest Canada. Often, the only opportunity to see them on this continent is during the summer months in Alaska. Such species include the spectacled and Steller's eiders, the bar-tailed godwit, the long-tailed jaeger, the bluethroat, and the white and yellow wagtails. The arctic warbler nests in central and western Alaska and winters in tropical Asia. It has a voracious appetite for mosquitoes.

Some species nest only in the Arctic or sub-Arctic, although seasonally common elsewhere in North America. Watching these birds in Alaska offers opportunities to observe behavior not seen elsewhere. For example, only on the breeding grounds do the Lapland longspurs produce their beautiful breeding song and perform their curious helicopter-like flights. The male and female divide their fledglings equally and care for them separately.

Some birds find their way to Alaska by accident. Because of violent storms or navigational errors, members of Old World bird species visit Alaska occasionally or on a regular basis. Spotting these vagrant birds is an exciting and unique experience. Examples of such species include the dusky thrush, the spoonbill sandpiper, the Chinese egret, and the great knot. Sometimes spotted in Alaska is the rare Steller's sea-eagle, which breeds on the seacoasts of eastern Siberia and winters in China, Korea, Japan, and the Ryukyu Islands.

Parakeet Auklet.
K.R. WHITTEN

SAFETY AROUND BEARS AND MOOSE

Never underestimate an animal's potential to injure a human, especially if the animal is hurt, frightened, or defending its young, food, or territory. Avoid surprising—and frightening—bears by making noise when hiking, and stay away from fresh kills. If you are confronted by a bear, do not panic. Stop, speak calmly, and wave your arms to identify yourself as human. You may back away slowly, but stop if the bear follows.

If a brown bear attacks, curl up in a protective ball and play dead. If a black bear attacks, fight back vigorously. If a moose charges, run and attempt to get something—such as a tree or a building—between you and the animal. Never get between a mother and her young.

Avoid camping on animal trails or near areas where wildlife concentrate, such as streams. Hang food and personal toiletries at least 10 feet off the ground and away from your camp. Burn or carry out all trash to avoid attracting bears or other wildlife.

REMOTE TRAVEL TIPS

Research and plan your trip carefully. Some of the most exciting wildlife viewing opportunities in Alaska occur in isolated, remote areas with few, if any, amenities. Contact the Alaska Division of Tourism for general information and the agency noted under "Contact" in the site descriptions of this book for more specific information. Make reservations early; services may be limited.

Dress appropriately and bring layers of warm, waterproof clothing. Always carry supplies to last longer than you have planned to stay. Much Alaska travel is weather dependent and the weather may change quickly and drastically; you may be temporarily stranded. Pack spares: tires, money, food, film, etc. When in the wilderness, carry emergency survival gear—such as waterproof matches, fire starter, and a space blanket—separate from your main backpack.

Recognize your limitations. Consider guided tours for areas of special challenge. Make sure someone you trust knows where you are and when you are planning to come back, so that they can alert authorities if you fail to return. Carry standard first aid equipment, and learn how to recognize and treat hypothermia.

Respect the culture and privacy of Alaska Native peoples and their land. Recognize that fishing and hunting camps you may come across are essential to local residents' subsistence way of life.

Bring insect repellant, "bug jackets," and/or head nets. Alaska is famous for its mosquitoes, no-see-ums, and other biting insects.

Do not attempt to hike across mudflats or glaciers. These can be treacherous. Speak with authorities before trying to negotiate these types of terrain. On saltwater outings, always carry a tide table.

Purify water taken from streams and rivers. Although water may appear pristine, treatment is still recommended.

FOR TRAVEL INFORMATION

Alaska Division of Tourism, P.O. Box 110801, Juneau, AK 99811-0801; (907) 465-2010; Fax (907) 465-2287.

Alaska Public Lands Information Center, 605 W. Fourth Ave., No. 105, Anchorage, AK 99501; (907) 271-2737.

Alaska Wilderness Recreation and Tourism Association, P.O. Box 1353, Valdez, AK 99686; (907) 835-4300; Fax (907) 835-5679

Alaska Marine Highway System, toll free reservation line: 1-800-642-0066; TDD machine access: 1-800-764-3779.

SUGGESTED READING AND REFERENCE BOOKS

Alaska's Mammals: A Guide to Selected Species, Dave Smith (text) and Tom Walker (photos), Alaska Northwest Books, 1995.

Alaska Mammals, Jim Rearden, editor, Alaska Geographic, Volume 8, No. 2, 1981, Anchorage.

Alaska's Fish: A Guide to Selected Species, Robert Armstrong, Alaska Northwest Books, 1996.

Guide to the Birds of Alaska (fourth edition), Robert Armstrong, Alaska Northwest Books, 1995, WA.

Wildlife Notebook Series, Alaska Dept. of Fish and Game, State of Alaska, 1994, Juneau, AK (907) 465-4190.

A Field Guide to Animal Tracks, Olaus Murie, Peterson Field Guide Series, Houghton Mifflin Co., 1974.

Guide to Marine Mammals of Alaska, Kate Wynne, University of Alaska, Fairbanks, Sea Grant Program, 1992.

Bear Facts: The Essentials for Traveling in Bear Country (free brochure available at Alaska public land information centers).

Discovering Wild Plants, Janice Schofield, Alaska Northwest Books, 1989.

Alaska's Wild Berries, Verna Pratt, Alaskakrafts, 1995.

The Alaska Wilderness Milepost and *The Alaska Milepost*, Vernon Publications, WA. (published annually).

A Republic of Rivers, edited by John A. Murray, Oxford University Press, 1990.

Animal Tracks of Alaska, Chris Stall, The Mountaineers, 1993.

The Nature of Southeast Alaska, O'Clair, Armstrong, and Carstensen, Alaska Northwest Books, 1992.

A Field Guide to Birding in Anchorage, R. L. Scher, 1989.

A Naturalist's Guide to the Arctic, E.C. Pielou, University of Chicago Press, 1994.

WILDLIFE INDEX

This list includes some of the species of interest to Alaska wildlife viewers. Following the species are the site numbers of the sites in which they are most common. This list is not all inclusive.

Mammals

Bison 17, 42, 43, 52
Black bears 7, 12, 37, 39, 40, 41, 63, 66
Brown bears 8, 43, 44, 52, 53, 54, 56, 66
Caribou 41, 44, 55, 58, 61, 63, 66
Dall sheep 22, 27, 34, 44, 49, 61, 62
Lynx 27, 40, 55, 56
Moose 25, 32, 33, 37, 40, 44, 45, 49, 66
Mountain goats 9, 11, 17, 19, 21, 27, 39
Muskoxen 61, 62, 67, 68
Reindeer 59, 60, 67, 68
Sitka black-tailed deer 1, 8, 51, 53
Wolverines 39, 55, 58, 63
Wolves 1, 41, 44, 45, 56, 58, 61, 66

Marine mammals

Beluga whales 23, 28, 38, 55, 64, 67, 68
Bowhead whales 60, 64
Dolphins and porpoises 1, 2, 16, 39, 51, 68
Gray whales 51, 52, 53, 57, 58, 68
Harbor seals 4, 9, 12, 16, 38, 40, 51, 55, 58
Humpback whales 6, 11, 12, 16, 19, 39, 51
Orcas 1, 16, 19, 40, 51, 58

Sea otters 1, 18, 39, 40, 51, 58
Steller sea lions 2, 11, 19, 51, 56, 57, 60
Walrus 56, 57, 59, 64

Fish

Salmon 1, 6, 14, 15, 21, 25, 29, 30, 56

Birds

Arctic terns 26, 28, 32, 35, 36, 43, 66, 68
Arctic warblers 44, 65, 68
Bald eagles 1, 7, 8, 13, 19, 37, 40, 52
Ducks 1, 3, 6, 10, 14, 18, 47, 50, 58, 59, 62, 64, 68
Peregrine falcons 19, 47, 48, 49, 57, 62, 67
Geese 3, 10, 14, 18, 20, 26, 38, 50, 58, 68
Gyrfalcons 43, 44, 48, 62, 67, 68
Jaegers 43, 44, 51, 61, 62, 64, 67
Loons 20, 26, 30, 32, 35, 37, 41, 51, 61, 62, 64, 66, 67
Murrelets 2, 8, 12, 19, 51, 57, 60
Puffins 12, 39, 40, 53, 55, 57, 60
Sandhill cranes 3, 21, 33, 38, 41, 47, 65
Trumpeter swans 3, 5, 14, 18, 20, 33, 41, 58

Design, typesetting, and other prepress work by Falcon Press,
Helena, Montana.
Printed in Korea.
ISBN 1-56044-066-X

Cataloging-in-Publication Data

Sydeman, Michelle, 1959-
        Alaska wildlife viewing guide / Michelle Sydeman and Annabel Lund.
                p. cm.
        Includes bibliographical references (p.   ) and index.
        ISBN 1--56044-066-X (alk. paper)
            1. Wildlife viewing sites—Alaska—Guidebooks. 2. Wildlife
watching—Alaska—Guidebooks. 3. Alaska—Guidebooks. I. Lund,
Annabel. II. Title.
QL161.S93 1996   96-1233
599.09798—dc20   CIP

$1.00 from the sale of every Alaska Wildlife Viewing Guide goes to the Alaska
Wildlife Conservation Trust, managed by the Alaska Conservation Foundation.

FALCON, P.O. Box 1718, Helena, MT 59624